A History of
TIDWORTH
and
TEDWORTH HOUSE

A History of
TIDWORTH
and
TEDWORTH HOUSE

David J. Croman

Phillimore

1991

Published by
PHILLIMORE & CO. LTD.
Shopwyke Hall, Chichester, Sussex

© David J. Croman, 1991

ISBN 0 85033 812 3

Phototypeset by Intype, London
Printed by Chichester Press Limited

Contents

List of Illustrations

Acknowledgements

Firstly I would like to express my thanks to Brigadier J. F. Deverell O.B.E. for showing a keen interest in the preparation of this book and contributing the Foreword.

In compiling material I have consulted numerous sources including: the County Record Office at Winchester; St Catherine's House, London; church and parish records; the British Library; the reference libraries at Salisbury, Farnborough and Aldershot; the Prince Consort Military Library, Aldershot; and Andover Museum. I am particularly indebted to Mrs. Gillian Heath and the staff at Tidworth library for obtaining material from a variety of sources. Amongst the residents of Tidworth I would like to acknowledge the help of Mike and Val Reid and to express my special thanks to Mr. Edward Otway who takes such a keen interest in the development of the village and whose collection of historic material has been invaluable. Anecdotal accounts from the ex-manager of the Garrison Theatre, Mr. Ken Pickernell, have also provided useful background. My thanks are also due to Major William Naesmyth of Posso R.A. who appears to be related to a 17th-century owner of Tedworth House and who has provided me with useful historic detail.

The advent of word processors has meant that many authors now type their own manuscripts, and I count myself in this growing breed. Much of the correspondence and other associated material was, however, typed by professionals and I thank Mrs. Lilian Stokes and Mrs. Sheila Lee for their assistance. I am grateful to Cpl. J. A. Glasspool R.H. and Mr. Alan Mather for assisting me with photographic processing, to Major Leslie Bond R.A. for the loan of photographs from the Salisbury Plain Training Area archives and to Capt. Mat Matthews R.C.T. for arranging aerial photographs of Tedworth House. Finally, I would like to thank all those other individuals, which space prevents me from naming, who have provided me with information and advice during the compilation of this book.

Permission to use the following illustrations is also gratefully acknowledged: Plates 3 and 17, Hobnob Press; Plate 11, Lutterworth Press; Plate 21, Macmillan.

Foreword

by Brigadier J. F. Deverell O.B.E.,
Commander 1st Infantry Brigade

Since the army began to use Salisbury Plain as a major training area during the latter part of the 19th century, Tidworth has been a temporary home to hundreds of thousands of soldiers of many nations. To some it would have been a welcome relief from the rigours of a more hostile environment, to others a wet, cold and inhospitable area, far removed from the sunnier climes from which they had been transported.

Over the years Tedworth House has provided an elegant backdrop to those officers and soldiers who have used the parkland for their recreation. To those who spent periods under canvas in the grounds the grandeur of the house must have seemed in direct and mocking contrast to their exposed living conditions. Today the house is one of the army's most prestigious officers' messes, having as members the officers from the Brigade Headquarters together with officers from various army units in Tidworth. This is perhaps a far cry from the glories of the past as a private mansion but the house still provides valuable and important facilities for residents and visitors.

My own first experience of Tedworth House was as a boy attending a military tattoo in the late 1950s. The author takes us back further than that to identify its origins. There is evidence that the Tidworth area was settled and farmed in Neolithic times; later, the Romans occupied it as it lay close to important networks of communication. The present name seems to have been derived before the 10th century and the variations in spelling have resulted in the continuing difference between Tedworth House and Tidworth village.

The history of the house begins somewhat later and reflects especially the rise of the Smith family, who later became the Assheton Smiths, to a position of wealth and influence. Like all great houses it has its reported ghosts, particularly the 'demon drummer of Tedworth', a wild and vindictive poltergeist who is still celebrated today in the name of a local public house.

The first clear link with the army was the raising of a yeomanry troop by Thomas Assheton Smith III in response to the farm labourer riots in the 1830s. The troop was probably the first military unit to be based in Tidworth. The house was further connected with the army by the patronage of the Duke of Wellington who was a frequent guest of the Assheton Smiths. Thomas was one of the foremost Masters of Foxhounds of his generation and in the house there is still a painting which depicts the Duke at one of the meets.

As the 19th century drew to a close so did the story of Tedworth House as a private residence. Sold to the War Office in 1897 it has since been used mostly as an Officers' Club or mess, but not entirely. In 1942 the then commander of the British troops in the area offered it to Eleanor Roosevelt as a Red Cross Club. For the following three years the house resounded to the noise of American soldiers relaxing, and the smell of hamburgers cooking!

I am delighted that David Croman has produced such a lively and well researched book. Its wealth of history demonstrates that the house has been at the very core of the development of Tidworth over the centuries and is a place of far greater importance than many who stroll, jog or ride past the house might presume. The house and village have a fascinating past and this book will be of interest not just to the civilian and military population of Tidworth but to anyone interested in learning about the lives of the squire-archy in their country houses and the development of a small village into a major military garrison.

October 1990

The Demon Drummer of Tedworth. From Joseph Glanvill's book *Saducismus Triumphatus* (1683).

Preface

The aim of this book is to put on record a detailed historic account of the development of South and North Tedworth from the perspective of their manor houses, in particular Tedworth House. It is impossible to divorce the history of these manors from the development of the two villages, after all the powerful owners controlled the land and much of the lives of their workers and tenants. Without people a house is an empty shell; they breathe life into it. I have, therefore, included biographical details of previous squires and lords of the manor which describe their achievements, quirks and failings, their life at Tedworth House and their influence on the village itself. Events taking place in the country generally, which impinge on village life, are also included to help set the historical perspective.

Very little has previously been written about Tedworth House itself. Apart from a brief mention in N. D. G. James' excellent account of Salisbury Plain, *Plain Soldiering*, and a 19th-century account of a previous owner, I could find no other book on the subject. I was fortunate enough to live in the house for three and a half years, and so was able to carry out a detailed study of the building at first hand, building a dossier, putting together clues until pieces finally began to make sense. This led to the discovery of material which, I believe, has not previously been reported.

In deciding on the scope of this book I was faced with the problem of where to begin its history. I felt that most readers would like to know something of the early origins of the village, so I have included this, albeit fairly briefly, partly in the form of a chronology of important events. After the 17th century much more is known and this is reflected in the detail given as Part One unfolds. Part Two begins with the rebuilding of Tedworth House in the 19th century and leads up to the sale of the house to the War Department. Part Three examines the profound transformation of the village into a major military centre and takes us through to the present day. A second chronology summarises developments from the 17th–20th centuries. The book finishes with several appendices for those who wish to read more in depth about particular topics.

David J. Croman
Farnborough, October 1991

Part One – The Early Manors

Village Origins

Visitors to Tidworth are usually surprised to find that it is made up of two villages, and that until 1992 each village was situated in a different county. North Tidworth was located in Wiltshire, whilst South Tidworth was in Hampshire. Confusion deepens when they notice a sign off the main road in South Tidworth pointing to 'Tedworth House', an elegant Palladian mansion standing in fine parkland. Could there perhaps be a misspelling? To explain the difference it is necessary to examine briefly the origins of the village name. In a document of A.D.975 the name is recorded as Tudanwyrth, a century later Domesday Book (1086) records the village as both Todeorde and Tedorde; by the 13th century we find Tudewrth (1203) then Tuddeworth (1289) and the 14th-century Tedeworth (1362). Of course, many differences in spelling occurred in a society which was largely illiterate, but these variations do give an indication of the pronunciation then in use. In the 19th century both Tedworth and Tidworth were used, the former spelling normally to denote the mansion house and estate of South Tedworth. As the military garrison was established in the early part of this century, straddling both villages, Tidworth became the standard form. The house with its estate and hunt, however, retained the earlier spelling. The village name is derived from the Anglo-Saxon 'worth', meaning an enclosure of land round a homestead, linked to a landowner – probably a tribal chief – named Tuda. Thus originally it was 'Tuda's Homestead'.

Tidworth lies in an area of England close to famous ancient sites such as Stonehenge, Old Sarum and Danebury Hill Fort. There is evidence that a settlement has stood alongside the River Bourne, in the valley between Clarendon Hill to the west and Furze Hill to the east, for at least 3,000 years, making Tidworth one of Britain's oldest villages. Ancient relics have been uncovered and prehistoric tumuli, barrows and earthworks surround the village. Hampshire is noted for several groups of barrows or burial mounds, seven in number, known locally as 'Seven Barrows'; examples are at Burghclere, Stockbridge and South Tidworth. The 'Seven Barrows' of Tidworth lie about seven hundred and fifty feet north of the western edge of Aliwal Barracks. Bronze Age skeletons were uncovered in 1923, close to Tedworth House, in what is now the sports field just to the west of the Arcot Road/Humber Lane junction. Just over a mile to the north-west of North Tidworth, on a prominent knoll, stands the Iron Age hillfort known as Sidbury Camp. Its defences enclose an area of some 17 acres from which there radiate out boundary dykes, probably once marking the areas of former pasture and cultivation. At 735 feet, Sidbury Hill is the highest point on the Salisbury Plain.

Tidworth was farmed throughout the Neolithic. Bronze and Iron Ages as a small settlement. In Roman times it probably grew in size and importance because it lay near to a major crossroads in their network of communications. An important Roman road, the Portway, passing close to Tidworth, linked the Roman towns of Sorviodunum (Old Sarum) with the canton capital town of Calleva Atrebatum (Silchester). Silchester, lying about eight miles north of Basingstoke, is the only Roman town in Britain to have been fully excavated and has probably the finest example of a Roman wall as well as an impressive amphitheatre. Crossing the Portway near Tidworth was another great Roman road linking

Venta Belgarum (Winchester) with Cunetio (Mildenhall). Part of a Roman pavement was excavated in North Tidworth in about 1836 and removed to the British Museum.

During the last phase of Roman rule, about the fifth century, Germanic raiders sailed to Britain, taking the opportunity to invade and settle as the authority of Rome collapsed. Broadly three Teutonic races colonised various parts of Britain – the Jutes who settled in Kent and the Isle of Wight, the Angles, giving England its name, who moved into East Anglia, Mercia and Northumbria, and the Saxons who came to Essex, Sussex and Wessex. Indeed, these latter county names are derived from East, South and West Saxons. The Saxons plundered and destroyed most of the Roman villas and towns in Wessex, preferring to live in small settlements, typically lying along river valleys. as in Tidworth. Throughout the Saxon period of dominance, roughly the 7th–11th centuries, several manor houses co-existed in North and South Tidworth.

Each manor would typically have had three great fields under cultivation growing barley, corn, wheat and oats as the major crops. These huge unenclosed fields, which normally surrounded the village, were divided into separate strips and allocated to the tenants by the lord of the manor. The strips were ploughed and sown together with the same crop, as one field, by pooling of resources such as oxen teams. The typical length of a strip-plot became established at about two hundred and twenty yards, this being the distance a team of oxen could plough before needing to rest – this was a 'furrow-long' or furlong as it became known. The average width was about twenty-two yards which gave a total strip area of an 'acre'. Under the direction of the manor court a three-year rotational cycle was followed, with two fields used to grow crops whilst the third lay fallow, allowing the land to recover and cattle to graze. The wheat would have been ground in mills standing alongside the River Bourne. The Anglo-Saxon manors were usually crudely built of wood or even wattle, clay and thatch, so little evidence of their existence survives. It is almost certain, though, that one of these manor houses would have been on, or very near, the present site of Tedworth House, close to the river and the medievel South Tedworth church (now demolished – see Appendix I).

Despite its tiny population, rarely exceeding 300 until the arrival of the army in the 20th century, the village nevertheless became known to the monarchy and the highest in the land through the powerful owners of the Tedworth estate. By the ninth century Wessex, with its capital at Winchester, had become the leading Anglo-Saxon kingdom, having gained supremacy over all England. Not until after the Norman Conquest in the 11th century did the centre of English power move to London. The Earl of Wessex, who became King Harold II, was in possession of parts of Tidworth before his death in October 1066 at the Battle of Hastings. After the surrender of Winchester to the Normans it has been suggested that the Norman army passed through Tidworth as it progressed north. The Norman victor, William I (the Conqueror), crowned at Westminster Abbey on Christmas Day in 1066, imposed a new feudal system on England but was careful to preserve the old Anglo-Saxon way of life in the villages and homesteads.

Wishing to know the full scope and nature of his new kingdom so that taxes could be fairly assessed, William I ordered the Domesday Survey to be carried out in 1086. This was the most extensive record of land division, inhabitants and economic resources ever produced in England, or indeed the world, up to that time. It was organised from Winchester. The name is derived from the belief that its judgement would be as final as Doomsday. It remains a major historical resource and gives us the first real record of the land and inhabitants of North and South Tidworth. The manor is the main feature of Domesday Book, the name being derived from the French *manoir*, meaning 'residence'. Early manors were often quite small and crudely built, based around a working farm with all tenants paying rent to the lord of the manor or labouring for him as serfs. We know from the Domesday Survey that the villages had several important landowners at that time, including the Norman Bishop of Bayeux. Before him, North Tidworth was under Odo, William the Conqueror's half-brother and the Bishop of Bayeux for whom the famous Bayeux Tapestry was produced. It is also recorded in Domesday Book that South Tedworth church existed and that the district was not well wooded, as later. One entry includes a rather amusing comment, indicating a dispute: 'In [North] Tidworth [is] one virgate of land which Croc proved ought to belong to him; Edward holds it however'. A virgate was about thirty acres. Details of Tidworth's principal land owners from 1066 to 1650 are given in Chronology I.

1.   Burial Chapel in Church Lane, South Tidworth.

Despite their small size and isolated location, the Tidworth villages were known to city merchants, leading political figures and the royal court itself. Although South Tidworth was usually more sparsely inhabited than North Tidworth, its manor house was to make it the more prominent village through the power of successive lords of the manor and squires of Tedworth House. On the county border, between the two villages, was the tiny hamlet of Hampshire Cross, a part of Tidworth noted today for its lovely thatched cottages and old red telephone boxes, standing just north of the Oval sports ground by the side of the Bulford Road.

As Christianity replaced Anglo-Saxon paganism, the parish church became a focal point of village activity and the parson or rector became second in importance only to the lord or squire. In Tidworth, as elsewhere, the rector was given land (glebe fields) for cultivation and was able to collect tithes, a tax of one-tenth, from villagers to support himself and the church. Before a parish rector became fully established the monarch Henry II, in 1164, granted the tithes of South and North Tidworth to the nuns of Amesbury, who may have had a small convent in the village. Both North and South Tidworth parish churches were stone-built and medieval in origin, perhaps standing on the site of an even earlier wooden place of worship. The churches of Tidworth are described more fully in Appendix I. In nearby Salisbury building of the magnificent cathedral was begun in 1220 and completed in 1266, a remarkably short time for one of the finest examples of Early English architecture. The hill fort of Old Sarum was deserted in 1220 as the city of New Sarum (Salisbury) began to establish itself around the developing cathedral.

During the spread of the black death through England in 1348–9, some villages were almost wiped out. It is recorded that 18 out of 41 tenants in nearby Durrington died of the bubonic plague and in Tidworth itself no rents at all could be collected as it seems that all the tenants had died. It has been estimated that about a third of the population of Europe died of the black death during 1347–50. Particularly badly hit were the clergy who buried the dead; indeed, the incumbent of South Tidworth parish church himself died. As many as half the clergy in England may have been killed as the plague spread throughout the country. The agricultural economy of Hampshire was badly shaken, cities such as Winchester and Southampton were decimated and the Isle of Wight appears to have been practically depopulated. It took generations for the country to recover.

The black death was to remain endemic in London for more than three centuries, the last major outbreak being in 1665 when the 'Great Plague' swept through the city killing about a quarter of the population of 400,000. Charles II's queen Catherine, the daughter of the King of Portugal, moved with her royal court out of London into the country to try to escape the disease. She chose Wilton House, near Salisbury, the seat of the Earl of Pembroke, which lies just 15 miles from Tidworth. It is likely that Tedworth House, as one of a cluster of great mansions in the area, would have provided accommodation and entertainment for members of the royal household at this time. The Great Fire of London which devastated the city in 1666 helped to eradicate the disease by destroying most of the rat-infested slums.

From the time of the Domesday Survey up to the 16th century only one manor seems to have been recognised in South Tidworth; later three manors are recorded in the parish: the North, Middle and South Manors. It appears that the Middle and South Manors were together known as the South Manor, with the North Manor lying over the border in Wiltshire. The Zouche family was in control of North Tidworth during the 12th and 13th centuries. Originally spelt 'le Suche', the name Zouche is today retained in Zouch Manor and the Zouch housing estate of North Tidworth. One of the first families in Britain to be granted a peerage (1308), the Zouche line continues to the present day although the 18th Baron Zouche, James Assheton Frankland (1943–) who served as a Captain in the 15th/19th King's Royal Hussars, lives permanently in Australia at the time of writing. By an odd coincidence an earlier member of the Zouche family married into the Assheton family of Cheshire. More will be said later of this family which helped to form a famous dynasty at Tedworth House. In the villages there was little change in the feudal system under a manorial lord until the 15th century, when some enclosure of fields began, so that landowners could turn over arable land to pasture, allowing the keeping of sheep for the growing cloth trade.

By the close of the 17th century the manor of South Tedworth was regarded as a single estate. The actual construction date of the original Tedworth House has not been discovered, but when Thomas Smith bought the estate from Jane Ashburnham in 1650 a fine country house was already established. Much of the wealth of Tidworth and its attraction to successive landowners over the centuries came from the vast flocks of sheep reared on the hills around the village. Sheep were a sound investment providing meat, milk, cheese and that great trading commodity, wool. They were also used as walking dung-depositors to fertilise the thin layer of loamy chalkland soil found throughout the district. During the day they were released on the surrounding hills, but it was at night when they were enclosed in sheep-folds on fields under cultivation that they unknowingly did their work. The folds were moved across the fields, day by day, to provide an organised system of fertilisation.

Woollen cloth manufacturing was the biggest and most profitable industry in Britain and was to remain so until the 18th century. Even today, the Lord Chancellor sits on the Wool-sack – a red cushion stuffed with wool – which symbolises the importance of the medieval wool trade. The trade was largely controlled by the great Merchant Adventurers of England, who supervised each stage of manufacture from raw wool to the finished material. These were London-based traders who formed guilds and livery companies, such as the Drapers', Ironmongers' and Goldsmiths' Companies to control the dealings of merchants.

Enter the Smiths

Peter Smith of the Fishmongers' Company was a powerful figure in the City of London. His influence allowed his son Thomas to become quickly established as a city merchant. A member of the Skinners' Company, Thomas was a man of great wealth when he purchased Tedworth House in 1650. The Smith family was to stay in ownership of the house for more than 200 years. The first Squire Smith moved to Tedworth with his wife Jane and son John. Thomas had married Jane Robinson in 1608 with the blessing of her father, who was a member of the London Merchant Taylors' Company. Through the marriages of his other children Robinson became related to no fewer than three sheriffs of the City and seven lord mayors!

The British East India Company, formed by Elizabeth I on the last day of 1599, had gained a trade monopoly in the East and was becoming immensely successful and powerful. Thomas was related to six of its committee members, two of whom became Deputy Governors and another who became Governor. His connections, therefore, were impeccable as he established himself as a leading international merchant of the city of London. These city connections did Thomas Smith no harm at all, especially when added to his father's

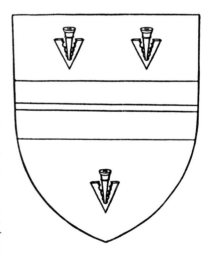

The Smith coat of arms.

already considerable influence. In 1629 Thomas was elected an Alderman of the City, granted arms and made a Master of the Skinners' Company. The Smith coat of arms, illustrated at Fig I, comprises 'Azure two bars between three pheons or' – pheons are barbed arrow heads.

By the time Thomas bought the Tedworth estate in 1650 his son John was already a prosperous landowner. Little is recorded about him, but we know from parish records that his son, also John, was born in Tedworth in 1655 and that his daughter Anne married Samuel Dashwood in South Tedworth church on 17 May 1670. The Dashwoods were also a wealthy family with city connections. Samuel himself was knighted in 1648, served as Member of Parliament for the City of London, and was Lord Mayor of London from 1702–3.

John Smith, grandson of Thomas, became the third of the Smith dynasty to own Tedworth House. He was to become a famous political figure of his time, entertaining the rich and powerful at Tedworth and helping to establish the estate as a country seat of considerable standing. As a young boy of seven years he would no doubt have been frightened by the reports of ghostly happenings at the nearby house of Mr. Mompesson (possibly Zouch Manor, North Tedworth). It became the first poltergeist disturbance to be thoroughly investigated, gaining national notoriety as the story of the 'Demon Drummer of Tedworth'. Even today *The Drummer* public house, just off Station Road, serves to remind us of the strange events which lasted from March 1661 to April 1662 (some reports say 1662–3, probably because of the changed calendar). Wild and noisy disturbances began in the house after a drum, said to have been confiscated from a travelling showman named William Drury, was sent to the Mompesson house by a local magistrate, John Mompesson, who was probably a relative of the house owner. The sound of loud drumming was heard all over the house and it got worse when the instrument was destroyed. It would sometimes go on for five nights in succession. Unusually for poltergeist phenomena some noises seemed to come from outside, above the roof, and could be heard at some distance from the house.

Along with the drumming, objects were thrown around, chamber-pots raised and emptied and children were said to be lifted out of bed into the air. Sudden changes in temperature occurred in rooms throughout the house and books were hidden away. So persistent and serious did these events become that the Rev. Joseph Glanvill, chaplain to King Charles II and an experienced witchcraft investigator, came to Tedworth to witness the disturbances at first hand. He carried out an intensive survey with the full agreement of Mr. Mompesson, who was apparently a serious-minded, sober person. Witnesses were thoroughly questioned and Glanvill himself was present to view many of the apparently paranormal events at the house.

Glanvill was unable to say positively whether trickery was involved (there was evidence that some occurrences could have been faked) and no one ever came forward to admit that they had contrived it, although Drury himself, at a later trial, is said to have boasted that he was responsible. This seems unlikely, as his presence in the village would have been noted. The incidents were certainly spectacular and for a period put Tedworth in the public eye. The famous essayist, poet and statesman Joseph Addison (1672–1719), who started the *Spectator* in 1711, based a prose-comedy entitled *The Drummer – or The Haunted House* (1715) on the Tidworth disturbances. Glanvill's own account was set down in his *Saducismus Triumphatus* (1683), extracts from which are to be found in Sir Richard Colt Hoare's *History of Modern Wiltshire*, published in 1826.

Since that time the story has passed into local folklore and a military drummer has become the Tidworth village symbol. Whilst all these remarkable happenings were taking place in the village John Smith the younger was setting forth on his education. He progressed to Oxford, leaving the University in 1672; two years later he was admitted to the Middle Temple. He made up his mind to pursue a political career, beginning it by representing the rotten borough of Ludgershall from 1678–89. During this period, in about 1684, he married Anne, daughter of Sir Thomas Strickland. The Stricklands were an ancient family who could trace their descent back to 1007 from the lords of the manor of

Boynton. They included William Strickland, who had travelled to the New World with Sebastian Cabot on his 16th-century voyages of discovery.

It is known that John and Anne Smith had at least five children, including three sons. Two sons, Thomas and Henry, appear to have died in childhood leaving the remaining son, William, finally to inherit the Tedworth estate. A daughter, Harriet, was, as we shall see, also to play an important part in the unfolding history of the village. John Smith continued to establish his political career, becoming Whig M.P. for Beeralston in Devonshire (1691–5), then representing Andover from 1695–1713. In May 1694 he was made a Lord of the Treasury, just three months before the opening of the Bank of England. He remained at the Treasury until being appointed Chancellor of the Exchequer on 15 November 1699, a post he held until March 1701. Between 1701 and 1705 he was out of office but remained an influential political figure with powerful friends such as the Lord High Treasurer, Earl Godolphin, and the Duke of Marlborough, both of whom undoubtedly helped him to become Speaker of the English Parliament.

Much controversy surrounded his appointment as Speaker in October 1705, where he won a bitterly-fought contest against Bromley. It was a 'night of the long knives' with, it is said, 15 office-holders who voted against him losing their posts. The Right Hon. Speaker John Smith continued to manage his estate at Tedworth whilst holding high office. He was re-elected Speaker without opposition in 1707 but, following the Act of Union in that year in which he had been involved as Commissioner, England and Scotland were now joined as Great Britain. Consequently he was Speaker of the first British Parliament – hitherto there had been separate legislative chambers.

Some measure of his standing with the monarch Queen Anne (1702–14) can be gauged from the gift she made him of the Snowdonian estate of Vaenol, which had reverted to the crown on the death of the previous owner. The estate, of some 47,000 acres, included an elegant country house on the banks of the Menai Straits and huge expanses of wild country around Mount Snowdon. The estate was to provide later generations of the Smith family with a substantial income from the Llanberris Slate Mines. Following his resignation as Speaker in November 1708 he was once again appointed Chancellor of the Exchequer. We can imagine how valuable were his important city connections with financiers and merchants. Even after his retirement from politics in 1710 he was appointed one of just four Principal Tellers of the Exchequer which brought an incredible income, equivalent to £1,500,000 in today's currency.

John Smith still held this position at the time of his death at Tedworth House on 30 September 1723; he was buried in the old South Tedworth church near to his father. Lady Anne Smith continued to manage the estate until her death at Tedworth on 1 November 1727. Ornate marble tablets were put up in their honour c.1730 in South Tedworth church by their fourth son Henry. These were subsequently moved to the Burial Chapel in Church Lane where they can be seen today. Thus ended a period when Tedworth was associated with the highest levels of national politics and the house, through Speaker John Smith, became known as a centre of hospitality to many of the most prominent and distinguished personages in the land. Speaker Smith's son Thomas inherited both the Tedworth and Vaenol estates as well as land in Collingbourne Kingston. Just five years later, however, he died, passing his inheritance to his brother William, the sixth son. Captain William Smith, an army officer, had now to devote himself more and more to estate management, becoming a distinguished country gentleman and a great landowner. He purchased Sutton Scotney Manor and estate in 1740, together with another manor in Wonston near Winchester. By a strange coincidence some of the Sutton Scotney land had been held by Robert, son of Gerald, during the period of the Domesday Survey when Robert had also held the South Tedworth estates. William's elder sister Mary married the second son of the Earl of Pembroke in 1705. Her husband, Robert Sawyer Herbert, became M.P. for Wilton, holding the seat for no less than 47 years. He lived in Highclere Castle about fifteen miles north-east of Tidworth but worked away for much of the time so Mary lived at Tedworth House for long periods. Highclere Castle, now the largest mansion in Hampshire, was at that time a big square classical house which had been built for Mary's husband Robert. His nephew Henry Herbert became Earl of Caernarvon in 1793 and Highclere Castle has remained the family seat of subsequent Earls of Caernarvon to the present day. Mary became a Lady of the Bedchamber to George II's queen, Caroline of Brandenburg-Ansbach, who exerted a considerable influence over the king, assuming the power of regent during his absence abroad. Mary was chosen to be lady-in-waiting at George II's coronation at Westminster in 1727, wearing a 'dress of blue and silver with a rich embossed trimming'. Queen Caroline died following an operation for rupture, looked after until the end by Mary as a lady-in-waiting.

The Assheton Connection

It was William's other sister Harriet who was to provide continuance of the family name through collateral descent. This may be seen more clearly by referring to the Smith pedigree chart at Table I. She married Thomas Assheton of Ashley Hall near Bowden in Cheshire on 6 May 1724 at South Tedworth church. The Assheton family had a long and distinguished history as the feudal lords of Assheton-under-Lyne. This history could be traced back to Ormus Magnus the Saxon Lord of Heletune and founder of the Church of Ormskirk and to Sir Ralph Assheton 'The Black Knight of Assheton' who had been knighted on the field of battle in 1482, a year before being made Vice Constable of England. During the first Jacobite Rebellion in 1715, when attempts were made to continue the Stuart monarchy by establishing James II's son, also James, as king, a meeting was held in Ashley Hall attended by the most influential men of Cheshire to discuss the crisis. It is said that Thomas Assheton gave his casting vote in favour of the House of Hanover thus supporting the monarchy of George I (1714–27) which has direct connections with today's royal family.

Thomas Assheton was Governor of Chester Castle when he married Harriet; they continued to live in Cheshire as William was still in possession of Tedworth House. Thomas and Harriet had six daughters (names unrecorded) and a son, also named Thomas, who inherited the Ashley Hall estate in 1759. He also inherited the Tedworth estate in 1773 on the death of William, who had been the last male in line of the Smith family but had been childless. Thomas Assheton the younger assumed the additional name of Smith after the death of William, becoming Thomas Assheton Smith the First. He planned to move to Tedworth House but was never to take up residence, dying in 1774 just a year after receiving his inheritance. His eldest son Thomas Assheton Smith II (1752–1828) was now in possession of both the Tedworth and North Wales estates and it is believed that he moved to Tedworth House with his six sisters at about this time. His younger brother William Henry was left the Ashley Hall estates which he held until his death in 1839 when, again having no natural heir, the property reverted to his nephew Thomas Assheton Smith III who finally sold Ashley Hall in 1846 to Mr. (later Lord) Egerton of Tatton Park.

Thomas Assheton Smith II was a formidable character known for his 'inflexibility of response' and often gruff manner. His stubbornness was said often to border on obstinacy. A keen sportsman and well-known fox-hunter, he firmly established himself as the next squire of Tedworth, taking a great interest in village life and the interests of his staff and tenants. Member of Parliament for Andover from 1797–1821, he also became Lord-Lieutenant of the County of Caernarvon through his ownership of the Vaenol estate in North Wales. A great landowner, his properties also included the Sutton Scotney estates and houses in London. During his management of the Vaenol estate the Llanberris slate

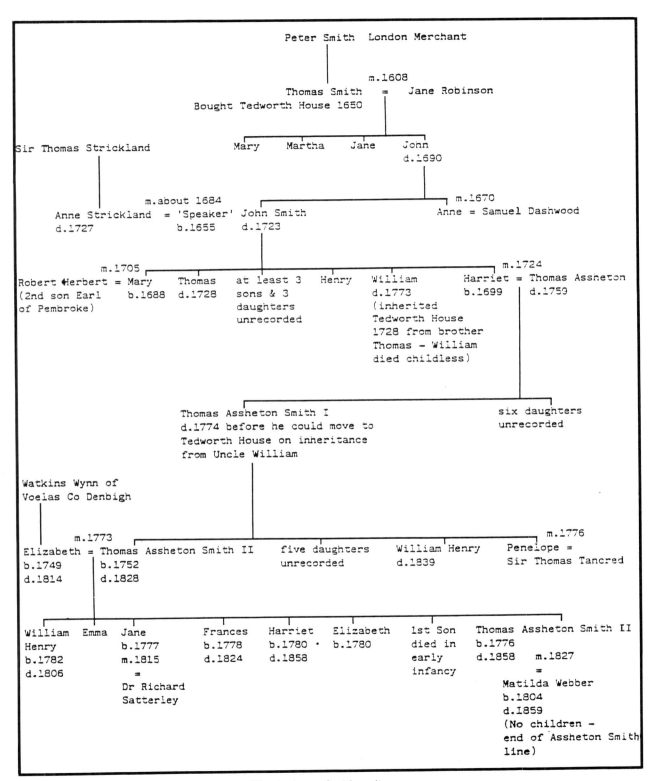

The Assheton Smith pedigree.

mines began to develop into a productive industry, providing him with an increasing income.

His Welsh credentials were further strengthened by his marriage to Elizabeth, a daughter of Watkins Wynn of Voelas, County Denbigh. They spent their time between the Tedworth and Welsh estates, probably visiting the latter mainly in the summer season. Thomas and Elizabeth had eight children, five daughters and three sons; one of the boys died in infancy (*see* Assheton Smith Pedigree at Table 1). Of the five sisters, three were married: Jane to Dr. Richard Satterley (Doctor of Physic) in 1815, Elizabeth to Major William Buckler Astley and Emma who became Mrs. Illingworth and subsequently Mrs. Jervis. The other two sisters, Frances and Harriet, died unmarried. Assheton Smith's second sister, Penelope, had moved to Tedworth House following the death of her father. She was married to Sir Thomas Tancred, Bart. at South Tedworth church on 8 October 1776 by special licence. Another family event held at the church was the marriage of Assheton Smith's sister-in-law, Jane Wynn, to the Hon. Charles Finch on Boxing Day 1778.

South Tedworth church, dating from medieval times, stood by the side of what is now the A338 near to the present site of St Mary's church. It was demolished in 1784 leaving South Tedworth and the Assheton Smiths without a place of worship (the background to this is described in Appendix I). Thomas decided to build a small family chapel in its place using stone from the demolished church. This building still stands as the Burial Chapel in Church Lane. During the building of his chapel, Assheton Smith II paid for pews for his family and staff in the North Tidworth parish church of Holy Trinity. As a consequence of the loss of South Tedworth church no records exist of burials or baptisms in the village from February 1784 to October 1785. The South Tidworth parish records go back to 1599, but those for North Tidworth are lost before 1700. A pedigree chart of the Assheton Smith family has been compiled from these records and other sources (Table I). Assheton Smith II's son William Henry was a Royal Navy officer who had distinguished himself at the Battle of Trafalgar in October 1805. Just a few months later he tragically died at sea. An epitaph, still to be seen today, was placed on the wall of the Burial Chapel. It reads:

> To the Memory
> of
> William Assheton Smith
> Second (surviving) son of
> Thomas Assheton Smith, Esq.
> of Tedworth.
>
> He was bred to the sea,
> and was Lieutenant of the Temeraire
> in the Battle of Trafalgar;
> in which by his bravery and conduct
> he contributed to that glorious victory.
>
> On his return to England
> he was appointed to the Namur:
> when being at anchor near St Helen's
> a boat with four men in it,
> belonging to a ship,
> got adrift in a violent gale.
> His humanity, equal to his bravery,
> urged him to leap into another boat
> for the purpose of saving them.
> But in the generous attempt
> he with seven men lost their lives,

on the 16th of January, 1806,
in the 24th year of his age.
To record the virtues of a beloved and gallant son
this marble is set up.

BY HIS AFFLICTED FATHER.

His ship was later immortalised by Turner in his famous painting *The Fighting Temeraire*
(1838) which recorded the vessel's last journey up the Thames to be broken up. The
painting now hangs in the National Gallery.

North and South Tidworth experienced annual flooding by the River Bourne for many
years right up to this century. A particularly severe period of flooding is recorded in North
Tidworth church records for the years from 1809 to 1828 when virtually every year 'the
water entered ye village and passed thro in great force'. High water levels usually lasted
from January until about June. Amongst many documents held in the County Record
Office concerning the Assheton Smith family is one of 1809 in which Assheton Smith II
makes a settlement to his son Thomas of £1,000 per annum, a substantial sum for the time.
It is possibly no coincidence that Assheton Smith II was able to make this allowance just

2.   The newly-built Tedworth House in 1833.

a year after selling his Sutton Scotney manor. When Thomas the elder and Thomas the younger jointly sign documents the latter uses the suffix 'Jnr'.

An early squire, probably Thomas Assheton Smith II, planted Assheton Coppice (now Ashdown Copse) just half a mile to the south-east of Tedworth House, below Furze Hill. It was in this woodland on the night of 9 December 1821 that a tragic event occurred. Under a full moon seven of Assheton Smith's gamekeepers, three of them armed, hid amongst the trees on the watch for poachers. Hearing a shot about fifty yards away they headed in that direction and encountered five poachers who, ignoring a warning, began to grapple with the keepers. The fight, lasting about half an hour, left one of the keepers, Robert Baker, lying shot dead on the ground. In the darkness and confusion all the poachers got away, making their way across fields back to Andover.

Two of the poachers were quickly caught, and a massive reward of £100 was offered for the capture of the others. The missing three, two of them from a well-known Andover family of bricklayers, were never caught. One of the captured men, Edmund Steele, turned king's evidence against fellow poacher James Turner, stating that Turner had pulled the trigger. James Turner was almost certainly innocent and denied the charge to the end, believing the murderer to be one of the two Goodalls who had led the expedition. James Turner was found guilty of wilful murder and hanged on the wall of Winchester County Gaol at 8.30 a.m. on 11 March 1822. His body was ordered to be surgically dismembered.

Just before this time Thomas Assheton Smith II handed over his parliamentary seat to his son Thomas the younger. The old squire had held the Andover seat for nearly a quarter of a century. The early 19th century saw the beginning of the steady decline of the woollen cloth industry. During the Napoleonic War there had been no competition from France, much business to be done with Government suppliers and strong order books. With the end of the war in 1815 orders were drastically reduced, the market became depressed and many cloth workers were laid off. As flocks of sheep were reduced in Tedworth Thomas Assheton Smith II no doubt saw a greater potential emerging in his North Wales slate mines which were beginning to employ hundreds of workers.

The great Weyhill Sheep Fair, held on Weyhill Down just outside Andover each year at Old Michaelmas, was reputed to be the largest in England where as many as half a million sheep were sold during the week. Sheep were driven to the fair from as far away as Warwickshire and a phantom village of fair booths stood on Weyhill Down throughout the year in preparation for the huge event. It dealt in men as well as livestock, with farm workers selling their labour. As this function grew it later became known as the 'Hirer's Fair'. Many labourers gathered in the town of Andover during the fair and there was a growing problem of gang disturbances which was to lead to the riotous events shortly to be described.

Weyhill Fair can be traced back to 1225 in the reign of Henry III. It was originally held each year on 29 September but in 1752 the Julian Calendar changed to the Gregorian version which is in use today. Eleven days were dropped from the calendar and in succeeding years the fair began on 10 October. Until the 19th century 'wife selling' was also practised at the fair, as husbands tried to dissolve their marriages by public auction. An example of this at Weyhill Fair is given in Thomas Hardy's *Mayor of Casterbridge* where a wife and daughter are sold. The last Weyhill Fair was held in 1957.

As well as sheep, other agricultural produce had commanded high prices during the Napoleonic Wars, which in turn stimulated greater production and increased prosperity for farmers who had benefited from Acts of Parliament allowing the enclosure of land previously farmed on the medieval open field system. Arable fields on common or manorial land became enclosed into self-contained farms which began to practise new cultivation methods, introduce mechanisation and improve the variety of livestock and crops. This prosperity did not, however, reach the labourer who continued to be poorly-paid and badly-housed, even when working on a successful farm. His wife and any children over the age of five were also expected to provide labour, the children being unpaid. Labourers' wages had actually fallen from an average 12 shillings a week in 1814 to seven shillings in 1830. Those in Wessex were some of the lowest in the country.

A wave of dissent began in the first quarter of the 19th century in protest against extreme poverty and miserable living conditions. This was to culminate in large-scale civil unrest. In 1826, during his famous *Rural Rides*, the great traveller and journalist William Cobbett journeyed from Marlborough to Salisbury recording that he saw 'the worst used labouring people upon the face of the earth. Dogs and hogs and horses are treated with more civility'. During this period of growing unrest the old squire of Tedworth, Thomas Assheton Smith II, died at the age of 77 years and was buried at Tedworth on 19 May 1828; he had outlived his wife Elizabeth by 14 years. Two years earlier his surviving son Thomas had taken up residence at Penton Lodge, Penton Mewsey near Andover. A year after he came to Penton, on 29 October 1827, he married Matilda, one of the famous Webber sisters of Binfield Lodge, Berkshire. Thomas Assheton Smith III decided to continue living at Penton following his father's death whilst he arranged for Tedworth House to be almost completely demolished and rebuilt to his specification. It is this house, built between 1828 and 1830, that still stands today.

Chronology One – Tidworth's Early History

This chronology is not exhaustive but gives brief details of the principal owners of the North and South Tidworth estates, together with significant events in the village, from the 11th–17th centuries.

1066–85
King Edward the Confessor and King Harold II are the first recorded lords of the manor of South Tidworth. Both died in 1066. After their deaths Cuthwulf held Harold's land, Alwin and two Freemen held Edward's land. In North Tidworth land was held by Odo, Bishop of Bayeux (Edwulf held it before 1066), Edward of Salisbury (Alfward before 1066) and Croc the Huntsman.

1086
Domesday Survey records South Tidworth's three estates as held by Hugh of Robert, son of Gerald, by Robert himself and by Croc the Huntsman (an Officer of the King and Warden of the Royal forests). Under Robert's holding Domesday Book lists a church; this was old South Tedworth church demolished c.1784. In North Tidworth, estates were held by Croc the Huntsman, Sheriff Edward of Salisbury (ancestor of the Earls of Salisbury) and the Bishop of Bayeux. Population of each village was about thirty people.

1174
Tithes of North and South Tidworth granted to nuns of Amesbury.

12??
King John granted the South Tidworth estate to Hubert de Burgh (Earl of Kent). For most of the 12th and 13th centuries the manors of North Tedworth appear to have been in the Zouche family.

1228
South Tidworth back under control of monarch (Henry III).

1270
William le Dun granted possession of South Tidworth. Charter given to him for a weekly market to be held at his manor each Monday and for an annual fair to be held on the vigil, feast and morrow of Holy Trinity.

1286
William le Dun died about this time, his son John in dispute with others to gain estate. Eventually stayed in le Dun family.

1316
John le Dun recorded as being in possession of the 'hamlet of Tidworth'.

1332
John le Dun died. Nicholas De Wyly inherited ownership of South Tedworth estate.

1337
Roger Norman in ownership of South Tidworth estate.

1348–9
Black death reaches Tidworth – all manor tenants appear to have died. No rents could be collected. Roger Norman died in 1349, his grandson Giles inherited the estate.

1362
Giles died, no immediate heir.

1373
Eventually South Tidworth Manor assigned to Julia Cavendish, who became Julia Shonne on re-marrying c.1375.

1391
Estate in hands of Alice Becket, the daughter of Julia Shonne by her first marriage, and her husband Richard Becket.

1411
On the death of Richard Becket the estate was inherited by his daughter Joan, wife of Robert Peny.

1428
South Tidworth estate was held by trustees, including members of the Peny family.

1484 The Dale family (William, then John) owned the North, Middle and South Manors of South Tidworth.

1496 The Sotwell family in control of North Tidworth. Thomas Sotwell was squire from 1496–1531; his son William succeeded him.

1522 John Dale died leaving a daughter Alice (aged 9 months) to inherit. She later married John Cooke who took control of the South Tidworth estate.

1550 About this time the Mompesson family had North Tidworth. They were to be influential in the village for over 100 years, being involved with 'Drummer' poltergeist disturbances of 1661–2.

1564 William Dale, brother of John, attempted to recover the South Tidworth manors as Alice had died without issue. Claim rejected and John Cooke continued in possession until his death in 1568.

1568 George Cooke, John's son, inherited manors.

1575 William Paulet (3rd Marquess of Winchester) in possession. His wife Agnes later inherited the South Tidworth estate.

1601 Agnes, Marchioness of Winchester, died leaving the lands to her daughter Katherine, who married Sir Giles Wroughton.

1622 Sir Giles and Lady Katherine quitclaimed the three manors to Sir James Ley, Bart., a judge and M.P. for Westbury. Sir James Ley became Lord Chief Justice of England, Speaker of the House of Lords, Lord High Treasurer, President of the Council and Earl of Marlborough (1626).

1629 Earl of Marlborough died – his third wife Jane inherited property. Jane later married William Ashburnham, the king's personal treasurer.

1650 Jane Ashburnham sold the South Tedworth estate to Thomas Smith, who established a family dynasty which was to last for over 200 years.

Part Two – A House New-Born

Riots and Rebuilding

During the period of the rebuilding of Tedworth House, farmers suffered two bad winters and poor harvests which created even more abject poverty for the labourers. In November 1830 the Swing Riots occurred, named after a mythical 'Captain Swing', who was said to be organising the farmer-workers. Farmers throughout the south received letters from 'Captain Swing', threatening them with arson and violence if they continued to use farm machinery instead of manual labour.

3.   'Captain' Assheton Smith parading his troop of yeomanry in Andover High Street *c.*1836.

Acts of machine breaking, rioting and fire-raising by roaming gangs of labourers broke out, beginning in Thatcham, near Newbury, then spreading rapidly throughout the region reaching Andover by 19 November, where some of the worst damage in the county was caused. The Labourers' Revolt reached its peak in Wiltshire on 23 November when 25 towns and villages were affected. Hayricks were a favourite target for arsonists and much damage was done to threshing machines. At Pyt House, a mansion near Tisbury, a troop of yeomanry was called to engage a group of about four hundred rioting labourers who

16

demanded higher wages. One labourer was shot dead. In Andover the 9th Lancers were called in to restore peace after rioting and vandalism got out of control.

Offenders were severely dealt with. In the County Courts at Salisbury and Winchester 153 were sentenced to death and another 269 to be transported for life, although in the event only four were actually executed. Few villages escaped the effects of the riots and there was certainly rick-burning around Tidworth village. So concerned were the squirearchy that they approached the Duke of Wellington for permission to raise a troop of Yeoman Cavalry to quell any local rising. The Duke readily agreed, having himself been attacked by fire-raisers in the recent riots at his Stratfield Saye estate. The troop was raised under the command of 'Captain' Thomas Assheton Smith III and inspected in Tedworth Park by the Duke himself, who praised their soldierly bearing and efficiency. Following the review the troopers, mainly local farmers and tenants, were entertained at Tedworth House. It could be said that these troops were probably the first to be based in Tidworth. Assheton Smith could not have imagined what part his house and the village were to play in military history.

The disturbances were put down in a matter of weeks and by early December 1830 the last of the great agricultural riots to be seen in the South of England were under control. With little improvement in wages or working conditions dissent still lay near the surface, leading in 1833/34 to some workers at Tolpuddle near Dorchester attempting to create a Friendly Society of Agricultural Labourers. Six labourers were charged with forming a Trade Union and the local magistrate, perhaps remembering the Swing Riots, meted out sentences of transportation, which created a public outcry. Agitation eventually led to the return to England, after two years, of the six Tolpuddle Martyrs.

Above what is now Station Road, on the top of Furze Hill which, at 596 feet, is the highest point in the village, an impressive double-turreted monument was built, known as the 'Observatory' or 'Round Tower' (see Plate 4). Its elevation allowed observers a complete view of the area surrounding the village. It was said that a barrel of tar was held on the top of the tower to be ignited if intelligence was received of the approach of a mob. A painting in the house of the Tedworth Hunt, hanging on the right of the fireplace in the central saloon, includes in the distance both the observatory and part of Tedworth House. When he was too old

4. The Observatory built on the top of Furze Hill, now demolished.

to hunt, Squire Smith was able to follow the progress of the hunt from the top of the Observatory. In the earlier part of this century the tower was used as private accommodation for estate workers at certain times. Sadly, the observatory was demolished at the end of the 1950s, leaving a massive pile of masonry rubble, some of which can still be found today. One villager collected some of the stone projections (corbels) which supported the battlements and made them into garden seats, thus preserving something from what was an interesting village 'folly'.

Thomas Assheton Smith III closely supervised the complete rebuilding of Tedworth House, moving there from Penton Lodge with his wife Matilda when work finished in 1830. Everything from the original building appears to have been demolished except for the old dining room which, against architects' advice, he insisted on retaining. It is believed that this dining room is the oak-panelled room which has lately become known as 'The Library'. It is quite different from the other reception rooms in the house, almost certainly dating from an earlier period.

Just up the hill to the west of the new mansion house the impressive stable block and kennels for foxhounds were completed to Assheton Smith's own design. They were to provide the base for what was to become one of the most famous hunts in Britain. By 1845 they housed 50 horses and 400 hounds for Squire Smith. The original stable block, built in 1829, is still largely intact, standing at the top of Stables Road. In 1991 it was being used as offices for the Department of the Environment's Property Services Agency. Within the central courtyard the old coach house can still be clearly seen but the jewel in the crown is the preservation of the Hack Stables. The original stalls and loose boxes stand on the old herring-boned stone floor, each stall having a horse's nameplate and being backed with the original porcelain tiling. As well as hack stabling, the block provided stalls for race-horses, hunters, post-horses and coach-horses. It also included a coachman's house, groom's house and mess room for stable lads. Water was drawn from a large circular well standing in the centre of the courtyard. Originally built just up the hill from the main stable block, the kennels proved unsuitable for the health of the hounds. A new kennel block was built on Home Farm, about ten minutes' walk from the house. Some remains of these kennels can still be seen in a building just off Humber Lane at Home Farm. The small existing stable block on the farm was also used by Assheton Smith.

Thomas Assheton Smith III (1776–1858), like his father, was a brilliant sportsman and a great rider. In fact, although proud of his son's horsemanship, the old man once confessed he was somewhat jealous of the boy's outstanding ability. Born on 2 August 1776 in Queen Anne Street, Cavendish Square, London, young Thomas grew up at Tedworth, enjoying country sports from an early age. At just seven years of age he was sent to Eton where he was the youngest boy. He spent 11 years there but in later life was to say: 'While there I learnt nothing'. One thing he certainly did learn was the 'noble art', fighting both inside and outside the ring throughout his schooldays. He loved fighting just for the fun of it and often quoted his personal maxim that if a boy were not well thrashed when he was young, he would probably need it when he became a man.

One of the most severe boxing matches ever witnessed at Eton was between Thomas Assheton Smith and another boy, Jack Musters. The contest lasted more than an hour and a half, finally being conceded as 'drawn'. The boys were so badly beaten that they 'could not distinguish each other'. On another occasion Thomas' temper got him into trouble with the law. An attorney who maintained that Assheton Smith owed him some fees, sent round his son, who acted as his clerk, to Thomas' Hyde Park house with a writ for the work done. A footman led the youth into Assheton Smith's study where, on hearing his mission, Thomas immediately struck him, knocking him to the floor. The following day Thomas received a summons to appear at Marylebone Police Court on a charge of assault.

5.　The principal entrance to the stable block, *c.*1840.

6.　The stable block today, now used as offices.

Still seething, he faced the charge, nearly committing a second assault during the proceedings, and was fined five pounds. An account of his court appearance was published shortly afterwards in the *Morning Post*. Many other anecdotes exist of his readiness to use his fists to settle a difference; even at 70 years of age he once jumped off his horse at Tedworth and prepared to fight a farm labourer who had thrown a stone at him as he passed. The man ran off! He also excelled at cricket, was an expert oarsman, an accomplished swimmer and played billiards to a professional standard. In 1802 he played cricket at Lords for Surrey against All England. From then until 1820 he played at county or national level in a distinguished cricketing career, appearing in the first Gentlemen v. Players match, held at Lords in July 1806, representing the Gentlemen (who unexpectedly won) with a score of 48 not out. He played for England in 1810 against Surrey finishing with the highest individual score of either side.

After leaving Eton he went up as a Gentleman Commoner to Oxford (Christ Church) in 1794 where he studied for four years. He actively continued his sporting pursuits, swimming regularly and rowing on the Isis. In his vacations he would arrange cricket matches at the excellent pitches on Perham Down followed by hospitality at Tedworth House. As soon as the cricket season was over, however, Tom Smith, as he became widely known, was back in the saddle for the start of the hunting season. This was very limited around the Tedworth estate until he cleared huge tracts of land following his father's death. Leaving Oxford in 1798, he moved up to Leicestershire where he quickly became known for his skilled horsemanship. Most of his energies were devoted to foxhunting and in 1806, at the age of only 30, he succeeded Lord Foley as Master of the Quorn, then the most fashionable pack in England. At the Quorn he took up residence at Quorndon Hall, his Mastership lasting for 10 years by which time he was regarded as the country's leading foxhunter. A contemporary poem, well known in hunting circles, included the verse:

> On Ajax, a nag well in Leicestershire known,
> See the gallant Tom Smith take a line of his own:
> Though in dirt fetlock deep, he ne'er dreams of a fall,
> And in mounting the hill, why he passes them all.

Giving up the Quorn on his move to Lincolnshire he almost immediately became Master of the local Burton Hunt which he held for eight seasons. Following this, for two years he hunted regularly with the Duke of Rutland's and other packs until moving to Penton Lodge, Penton Mewsey, just outside Andover in 1826. At Penton he set about forming a new pack, purchasing hounds from Sir Richard Sutton who had succeeded him at the Burton. A pack of extremely high quality was carefully chosen by Thomas with dogs selected from nearly 20 of the best kennels in England. His preparation was worthwhile as he was to hunt the district for the next 32 seasons.

Tom Smith was frustrated in his plans to clear the countryside around Tedworth for hunting by his father's opinion that it would be an act of madness. At that time there were few open rides; it was massively wooded, wild and scrubby and few people believed it could ever be made into satisfactory hunting country. Assheton Smith III had to wait until his father's death in 1828 before he could begin his grand plan to create a new palatial mansion in the centre of landscaped hunting country. No longer restricted by his father's objections, he mobilised an army of workers to remove hundreds of acres of woodland, cut rides through forest and landscape thousands of acres of land in and around Tidworth. He systematically gained agreement with surrounding landowners for them to continue laying the rides through their country or he leased the land from them and organised the work himself. This produced so much wood that Andover was said to look like 'a great timber mart'.

'The Richest Commoner . . .'

In 1830 Thomas moved his hunting establishment to Tedworth House, continuing his ambitious project to clear the country and commencing meets which were to become some of the most famous in England. Almost universally recognised as the most accomplished huntsman of his day, Tom Smith was fearless in the saddle. His riding skills were formidable; he would run at gates or hedges which no other rider would attempt. Most of the time he was successful but inevitably he was thrown many times, incredibly never suffering more than a few broken bones. He put this down to being a 'good faller', once remarking: 'All who profess to ride should know *how* to fall'.

The new squire opened up an area of about four hundred square miles of hunting country around Tedworth, bordering on the Craven Hunt to the north, the Wilton to the west, the Vine and Hursley to the east and the New Forest to the south. The north-western boundary was the Savernake Forest. So much open country now existed that runs of great length were possible in the chase. One of the most remarkable runs ever recorded under Assheton Smith's mastership took place in 1848. Beginning at Everleigh the hounds skirted Burbage and South Grove, ran through to Grafton Fields and Bedwyn Brails to Shalbourne Plantation. Heading next for Oxen Wood they turned back to Botley Clump, racing down to Martin and through Wilton Marsh where they picked up the fresh scent of a fox. The hounds had run a distance of some 25 miles, without being checked, in a time of 2 hours 25 minutes.

Assheton Smith III carried on the family tradition of being Member of Parliament for Andover, a seat he held from 1821 to 1832. Politically Thomas was of the old Tory school and resistant to change. A regular attender at debates, he supported his party in votes at every opportunity. He would hunt in the morning, then set off from Tedworth House after lunch for Parliament in a 'light chariot' pulled by four horses, travelling up the Avenue past the Lodge, climbing up Assheton (now Ashdown) Terrace then heading to London via Andover, taking his seat at Westminster for the evening session. By noon the next day he would usually be back at Tedworth in the saddle for the start of another meet. To put Assheton Smith's London journey in perspective, the famous Exeter mail coaches, considered to be the fastest in the land during the 1820s and '30s, travelled the 67 miles from Piccadilly to Andover in six hours.

He lost his Andover parliamentary seat as a result of his fierce opposition to the Reform Bill of 1832. The bill, passed by Earl Grey's Whig ministry, gave the vote to middle-class men and redistributed seats in favour of larger cities. Later that year he took up another seat as Member of Parliament for Caernarvon which he held until 1841. Following the loss of his Andover seat his heart seems to have gone out of parliamentary attendance, as he is seldom mentioned in the debates. He was still, however, an influential landowner with many powerful friends. On 23 March 1837 a sumptuous dinner was given to Assheton Smith by the Tedworth Hunt. Eighty-two gentlemen sat down in Andover Town Hall, which had been built just two years before at a cost of £7,000. The company at dinner included the Marquis of Douro, the Lords Frederick and William Paulet, Sir Edmund Antrobus, Bart. and the Mayor of Andover.

Said to be the 'richest commoner in England', he had an annual income equivalent to a million pounds in today's currency. His great wealth came from several sources, but in particular from his very productive slate quarries in Llanberris, North Wales. The nearby harbour of Port Dinorwic in the Menai Straits could berth 120 ships. From here thousands of tons of slate were exported world-wide, much of it in Assheton Smith's own fleet of vessels. By the mid–19th century the quarry railway was transporting 1,200,000 tons of slate annually. Thomas and Matilda normally spent the summer months at their North Wales estate, returning to Tedworth in the early autumn for cub-hunting.

7.   A rare picture of the conservatory and palm house built in 1845 on the east side of Tedworth House.

As might be expected, large quantities of slate were brought to Tidworth from Vaenol, incorporated into the house and used in the village. It was so abundant that it was fashioned into garden fencing which was quite a feature of the village and could still be seen until quite recent times. A long section of it can be seen running in front of the cottages in North Tidworth shown in Plate 16. Thomas kept a fleet of yachts at Vaenol, being somewhat ahead of his time in this rich man's leisure pursuit. His talents extended to boat design and it is said that he gave the Admiralty the initial idea for the first naval gunboat. He also claimed to be the inventor of a radical bowline design for his own ships which greatly improved their speed and passage through water.

His wife Matilda was childless and, perhaps because of this, devoted much of her time to the welfare of the village tenants and their children. By 1845 her deteriorating health was causing Thomas concern; she had been advised to go abroad for the winter but did not wish to leave Tedworth, so he decided to provide a Mediterranean climate for her within the house. He ordered the building of an enormous conservatory as an extension to the north side of the house, leading east. At the end was a magnificent palm house with steps leading down to a terrace. Throughout the conservatory, on either side of a gravel pathway, were lush plants, kept at tropical temperature by double hot water pipes. So large was the structure that Assheton Smith exercised his horse in it when his own health started to fail. This conservatory can be seen today, running behind the carriage porch, barely recognisable since the bricking up of the windows. It is now used as a corridor, kitchen and shower block. The floor and steps of the palm house still exist, forming the back of the east side tennis courts.

Despite his quick temper and obsession with hunting to the point of eccentricity, Thomas was prepared to help others in need. In 1847, after a rapid thaw following a deep frost, there was severe flooding in a whole line of villages along the valleys of the Salisbury Plain. Tidworth was inundated, leaving the inhabitants in a state of extreme privation. The squire immediately rode out and gave £100 for poor relief. Others followed his lead, with so much money being raised that a surplus could be given to Salisbury Infirmary. Many other examples exist of his generosity if he felt the cause just, and when Matilda approached him with plans for a village school he readily agreed. The Church of England Aided School was built at Hampshire Cross in 1857 with money provided by Assheton Smith. Taking 100 village children it was known as 'Mrs. Assheton Smith's School' for many years. A handsome, brick-built school, it stood at the bottom of Perham (now Station) Road at the junction with Pennings Road (A338) for over a century, being closed in 1950 and finally demolished, despite some local protest, in 1985. Eardley-Wilmot (1860) recalls that the sight of 'the girls in their red cloaks on a Saturday afternoon, and of the noisy urchins rushing from the porch to commence their various pastimes would suffice to gladden the heart of a *Times* commissioner'. Matilda died just two years after the building of her school but, following her wish, in 1860 her sister Harriet donated the huge sum of £2,000 to the school for its future maintenance. Many village children were to benefit from Matilda's generosity although compulsory education for all children was not required by law until the 1870 Education Act.

Other charitable works by Assheton Smith in the village included the repair and upkeep of the Tedworth Almshouses which had been built by Dr. Thomas Pierce, Rector of North Tidworth (1674–7), and later Dean of Salisbury. Standing on Zouch Manor Farm at right angles to the A338 just past the existing North Tidworth post office on the Marlborough side, the almshouses consisted of four substantial tenement blocks to house the poor. In 1691 they had been conveyed from Robert Pierce (son of Thomas) to 'Speaker' John Smith whose family continued to maintain them until Thomas Assheton Smith III's death in 1858. There was no formal national provision for the care of the poor and destitute until the Workhouse System was introduced by a Parliamentary Bill of 13 August 1834. This Bill, presented by the Prime Minister Lord Grey, and passed with a large majority, was a direct result of social reforms set in train following the Reform Act of 1832. It was this legislation which had led to Squire Tom Smith losing his Andover seat. He was therefore able to distance himself from the so-called 'Scandal of the Andover Workhouse' which broke in 1846 after many years of cruelty and degradation.

The Andover workhouse had opened in 1837, the first year of Victoria's reign and the year that Dickens' *Oliver Twist* was published. The 'scandal' involved the activities of the Workhouse Master, Colin McDougal – an ex-army Sergeant Major, who had been feeding the paupers a ration reduced even from the one which had originally been set at practically starvation level. McDougal had also been physically abusing the children and sexually abusing female inmates. He established a brutal work schedule keeping the emaciated paupers at 'bone crushing' until their hands bled. The abuses finally came to official notice leading to a public enquiry held in the House of Commons, which was reported widely, especially in the *Times* which was campaigning strongly against the Poor Law Commission. The pressure of public opinion led to the dissolution of the Poor Law Commission in July 1847. The scandal made Andover more famous than it had been since the time of the great Weyhill Fairs. The Andover workhouse building is still in use today as part of Cricklade College in Junction Road.

One of the best known farmers in the village, Thomas B. Northeast, farmed about seven hundred acres in North Tedworth and also acted as Squire Smith's agent. He and another village farmer, William Dowling, were the South and North Tedworth Elected Parish Guardians for the Poor Law Commission, attending meetings under the Andover Union to decide provision for the paupers. Each Union consisted of about thirty of the surrounding parishes. Payment day was Wednesday when the Relieving Officer visited South and North Tedworth to supply the paupers with bread from the back of a cart and with money at the Paupers' House.

8. Church of England aided school, Station Road, built for Mrs. Assheton Smith in 1857 and demolished in 1985.

Thomas Northeast died in 1840 and was buried in North Tidworth church where his impressive tombstone can be seen today just outside the south entrance. Assheton Smith is clearly mentioned on the side of Northeast's worn and faded tomb, often leading to the mistaken belief that this is actually Squire Smith's grave. William Dowling had South Manor Farm (580 acres); the rest of South Tedworth was farmed by Assheton Smith. Dowling also farmed North Tedworth together with Harry Sweetapple, Thomas Northeast, and Simon Tayler, each holding about seven hundred acres. As well as oats, barley and wheat many fields were given over to turnip growing. Thomas Northeast became well known for his breeding of Southdown sheep which had originated at Glyndebourne. A memorial tablet to William Dowling is on the south wall of the Burial Chapel in Church Lane.

In about 1845 a private gas works was installed close to Home Farm for house lighting. There was a gas generating plant and gas man's house. The latter, known today as 'Gas Cottage', is still occupied as a private dwelling. All that remains of the gas supply in

Tedworth House is a cupboard containing some of the original controls to the 'Servants' Office' and 'Chamber Floor'. Thomas was an amateur inventor and designer passing his plans for a mobile gun battery, which he said would be resistant to enemy artillery, to the Secretary of State for War, who was said to be interested in the idea. At Tedworth House, as well as in his London house and at Vaenol, Thomas installed another invention of his own, a kind of railway system between the kitchen and dining room which transported dishes back and forth enabling his servants to stay in the room between courses. Visitors to the house enjoyed first-rate hospitality with an excellent table and high standard of service. Thomas looked after his servants well and a major event at the house each year was the servants' Christmas Ball.

Although not a handsome man (he always maintained that the fight with Jack Musters had spoilt his looks) Thomas cut an impressive figure with his strong athletic frame and height of five feet ten inches. Thomas's usual dress for dinner was rather old-fashioned for the period – a blue coat with brass buttons and buff waistcoat, white silk stockings and black pumps. In the hunting season he would usually dine in scarlet, the inside of his coat lined with white silk. After dinner the men would often retire to the billiard room to play on the beautiful slate table where Thomas could demonstrate his skill. The Duke of Wellington, a regular visitor to the house and the hunt, was also an accomplished billiard player and they enjoyed many close matches. Assheton Smith and the Duke enjoyed a close friendship so when a rumour spread that Tom Smith had died, Wellington, who was in London, immedi-

9. Thomas Assheton Smith III, famous foxhunter and owner of Tedworth House.

ately sent the Marquess of Douro from Stratfield Saye to Tedworth to check the story. He found Squire Smith in good health. On receiving the good news Wellington sent the following letter:

London, Nov 12, 1851

My Dear Smith,
   They have killed you again in these last days! But I have been happy to learn that the report is without foundation.
   They treat you in this respect as they do me. I conclude that it is in your capacity of Field Marshal of Fox-Hunting.

Ever yours, most sincerely,
Wellington

Thomas Assheton Smith III probably did more to make Tedworth known than any member of the Smith dynasty. His reputation as a horseman was widely known – he was once addressed by Napoleon I as 'Le premier chasseur d'Angleterre' and Wellington said he would have made a first-class cavalry general. A master of hounds for over 50 years, he once estimated he had personally cut off the brushes of 1,500 foxes with his pocket knife. The 'lawn meets' at Tedworth House where, following a magnificent breakfast, foxhunters would assemble on the lawn outside the dining room, were famous throughout the hunting establishment. At the time of writing the Tedworth Hunt Ball is still held each year at the house.

An impressive event was organised at Rolleston in 1840 when Thomas was invited to join a 'Grand Meet'. More than 2,000 horsemen and women, including some of the most distinguished riders in the country, assembled to honour his contribution to foxhunting – probably the largest hunt ever to gather in Britain. Crowds of people thronged on to the plain to see the spectacle, which has never been repeated. Assheton Smith's love of yachting was clearly on display in the library (now the Green Room) where on ledges there stood models of his favourite steam-yachts – *Fire Queen*, *Glow-Worm*, *Jenny Lind* and *Sea Serpent*. Over the mantelpiece was a fine water-colour of *Sea Serpent*. He took a great interest in the design of boats and incorporated many of his ideas into his fleet. He owned and sailed several sailing and steam-yachts, some of them having his 'wave-form' hull design. Just after the Battle of Waterloo Thomas had sailed one of his yachts to Ostend where he took on board Lord Raglan (then Lord Fitzroy Somerset) who had lost an arm in the battle, bringing him home to a hero's welcome.

The Queen had instituted the Victoria Cross for acts of conspicuous bravery in 1856. One of the first medals to be awarded went to a nephew of Thomas Assheton Smith, Captain Clement Walker Heneage of the 8th Hussars (King's Royal Irish), for action at the Battle of Gwalior during the Indian Mutiny of 1857. Capt. Heneage (1831–1901) was a veteran of the Charge of the Light Brigade at Balaclava and had fought at Alma and Inkerman. At Gwalior he won his V.C. in action when, together with three soldiers, he helped to rout the enemy by charging through a rebel camp, capturing two enemy artillery pieces and delivering them to British lines under heavy cross-fire. He was the son of Matilda's sister Harriet, who was to provide upkeep for the village school after Matilda's death.

The old squire died at Vaenol on 9 September 1858 at the age of 82 following an illness. His body was brought back to Tedworth where it was interred in the churchyard of the Burial Chapel in Church Lane. All his possessions were bequeathed to his widow Matilda after his will was found on just a half-sheet of writing paper. Apart from a few legacies to servants Matilda was his only beneficiary. At Assheton Smith's death his kennels were well stocked with about one hundred and twenty couples of hounds. His wife presented these to the Tedworth Hunt which now had a new master, Lord Ailesbury. Matilda herself was suffering poor health and decided to spend the winter in Torquay. She rallied slightly but in the spring she fell severely ill and insisted on being taken back to Tedworth. She never completed the journey. On the way back she weakened further, so had to stop at Compton Basset, her brother-in-law George Heneage's residence near Devizes, where she died on 18 May 1859, just eight months after her husband, aged 55.

It had been planned to place the bodies of Thomas and Matilda (and Matilda's mother, who had died shortly before) in a mausoleum in the grounds of Tedworth House, but this had not been completed at the time of their death. On 26 May 1859 Matilda was buried instead alongside her husband in the graveyard of the Burial Chapel where their rather inconspicuous stone tablets stand today, at ground level on the left of the entrance, together with the stone of Thomas' sister Harriet who had also died in 1858.

There were no children from the marriage so Matilda left the Tedworth estate to her godson and favourite nephew, Francis Sloane Stanley. The Welsh estate at Vaenol she left to one of her late husband's nearest relatives, whom she had never met, the son of a Captain Duff, and grandson of Tom Smith's sister Elizabeth. The Smith squirearchy had come to an end after dominating the village for more than 200 years. One mystery remains however – why were no members of the family raised to a peerage or even given a title? 'Speaker' Smith had, after all, been a distinguished politician and later owners of Tedworth House had possessed immense wealth and been well-known by the establishment and monarchy. Were they perhaps almost too rich, regarded as mere trade merchants? Or were there other political reasons for this non-recognition?

Barons and Batsmen

The new owner of Tedworth House, Francis Sloane Stanley, lived at Leesthorpe Hall, Melton Mowbray; he was the son of the Rev. George Sloane Stanley and Laura Maria Webber. On receiving his inheritance in 1859 he declined to take up residence in Tedworth House, deciding instead to find a tenant. The first tenant was almost certainly Lord Broughton (John Cam Hobhouse 1786–1869), a well-known statesman. Created Baron Broughton de Gifford on 26 February 1851, he was made a K.C.B. on his retirement from political office in 1852. Attending the House of Lords only rarely, his last appearance in debate was during the Government of India Bill in July 1858.

Hobhouse then withdrew almost entirely from public life, spending most of his retirement at Tedworth House and at his town house in Berkeley Square. He did much writing at Tedworth House and would have entertained many of his numerous friends there. The precise dates of his occupancy are not known but he was still in residence in 1861. At Cambridge he had founded the 'Whig Club' and 'Amicable Society' and become a close friend of Lord Byron (1788–1824), the great romantic poet and exponent of revolutionary liberalism. Hobhouse travelled widely with Byron across Portugal, Spain and Gibraltar, then to Albania, Greece and Constantinople. He was 'best man' at Byron's wedding in 1815. Later they visited Rome and Venice together. Hobhouse also wrote the notes for the fourth canto of Byron's *Childe Harold*. Generally recognised to be Byron's most intimate friend, he was made an executor of his will and took responsibility for the poet's funeral arrangements in 1824.

In 1819, a year before being elected as Member of Parliament for Westminster, he was committed to Newgate Prison having been found guilty of breach of parliamentary privilege for his writings in a political pamphlet. He remained in prison for two and a half months, being released on the dissolution of Parliament. His maiden speech on 9 May 1820 was the beginning of his distinguished, if somewhat fragmented, career in the House of Commons. Early in his career he is said to have coined the phrase 'His Majesty's Opposition', still used today to describe the 'other side' of the House. Unlike Thomas Assheton Smith, John Cam Hobhouse was a firm supporter of the parliamentary reforms of the early 1830s. Succeeding his father as 2nd baronet in August 1831 he was made War Secretary the

10.   The south side of Tedworth House with the croquet lawn in the foreground.

following February. He was able to bring in many reforms including the restriction of flogging in the army to only certain proscribed offences. In March 1833 he became Secretary for Ireland, a post he was to hold for only a short time as he resigned from Government and Parliament over the abolition of the house and window tax.

On becoming Prime Minister in 1834 Lord Melbourne called Hobhouse back to the Cabinet as the first commissioner of woods and forests. When Melbourne was ousted at the end of his first year Hobhouse resigned once more. He was returned to Parliament at the General Election of 1835, becoming President of the Board of Control with a seat again in the Cabinet under Lord Melbourne. In this post he attended Victoria's first Queen's Council at Kensington Palace in 1837. After Melbourne's resignation in 1841 Hobhouse again left politics, but was called back in 1846 to resume his post at the Board of Control. He won back a parliamentary seat in a by-election in March 1848.

At Tedworth, and at his London house in Berkeley Square, Lord Broughton continued his writings and association with his numerous friends. Again Tedworth House was a centre of hospitality for the rich and famous. The actual dates of Lord Broughton's occupancy of Tedworth are not clear but he was certainly still in residence in 1861. He died after a short illness on 3 June 1869 at the age of 83, his barony becoming extinct, whilst his baronetcy passed to a nephew.

The second of Stanley's tenants was Edward Studd, a rich planter recently returned from India. He took the lease of Tedworth House and Home Farm on 16 June 1871. His son Charlie (C. T. Studd) was to become one of England's greatest cricketers and Edward himself was to bring about dramatic and unexpected changes to life at Tedworth House. A keen huntsman, Edward Studd was a master of hounds in Leicestershire where he lived in Hallaton Hall. He loved cards and the theatre, and had a passion for horse-racing, forming his own training establishment at Tedworth House soon after his arrival. He stabled about twenty racehorses and built a racetrack in Tedworth Park, enabling him to train his horses to a high standard. The pinnacle of his success was the winning of the 1866 Grand National at 40–1 with Salamander, a favourite horse. When Salamander later fell and had to to be destroyed, the Studd family came down to dinner dressed in black. Studd's horse Despatch gave him further success, taking second place in the 1871 Grand National.

Edward Studd's life underwent a fundamental change when, in 1876, he was persuaded by a friend to attend an evangelist meeting at the Drury Lane Theatre in London. The speakers were the famous American preachers D. L. Moody and D. Sankey, who were touring the country. What Moody had to say, in particular, transformed Edward Studd's thinking. He left the meeting dazed and exhilarated, resolving to spread the evangelist message himself. Back at Tedworth he shocked relatives and staff by selling his horses and giving up racing. He replaced much of the fine furniture in the house with benches and chairs so that he could hold prayer meetings in the hall on Sunday evenings. Each of his three sons was converted on the same day at Tedworth House by a visiting preacher. Tedworth House became something of an evangelist centre with Edward Studd inviting leading speakers to preach the Gospel to all who would attend. Studd's transformation was summed up neatly by his coachman who, when asked by a guest if his master had 'become religious or something', remarked, 'Well sir, we don't know much about that, but all I can say is that though there's the same skin, there's a new man inside'.

The boys Kynaston (J. E. K.), George (G. B.) and Charlie (C. T.) were all at Eton together and became the first three brothers to captain the Eton XI in successive years. This has only been matched by the Ashton brothers who were captains in turn 1921–3. C. T. Studd was made Captain of the Eton XI in 1879. Whilst at Eton they would return to Tedworth House for holidays, playing cricket there in the summer months on a former paddock which their father had turned into a first-rate pitch. Edward's third son, C. T., also fell under the spell of Moody and Sankey, attending many of their meetings and eventually going to China as a missionary, as will later be described. Edward Studd seems to have had a child late in life, in the year of his conversion, as the South Tedworth parish register records the baptism on 26 April 1874 of 'Reginald Augustus Studd son of Edward and Dora Studd of Tedworth House (Esquire)'.

Only two years after his religious conversion Edward's life came to a dramatic end. He had just left Tedworth House to travel to one of Moody's meetings when he stopped his carriage to go back to collect one of his grooms. As he ran back to the house he burst a blood vessel in his leg and shortly afterwards died. For two years he had only been concerned with 'saving souls', putting aside his love of horses, racing, the theatre and cards. He had ridden around the country urging people to come to his meetings and many hundreds had done so. At his funeral the clergyman said in his sermon that Edward Studd had done 'more in two years than most Christians do in twenty'.

C. T. Studd went up from Eton to Trinity College, Cambridge, where he gained his cricketing Blue. By 1883 he was Captain of the University Cricket Team, following in the footsteps of his older brother G. B. who had held the captaincy the year before. His other brother J. E. K. was Captain the following year – another first for the trio. C. T.'s

Cambridge career was described as 'one long blaze of cricketing glory'. He had his bats made one inch longer than normal to give extra leverage for his powerful wrist action. In 1882 he was rated the premier batsman in England. He made 118 runs for the Players against Australia, 100 runs for the Gentlemen v. Players at Lords, and 126 not out for the Players v. the Gentlemen of England. His bowling was only bettered by one other player (Peate). In the first match named above he was joined by his two brothers as the first pair of batsman. Through *Punch* magazine they became known as 'the set of Studds'!

C. T. Studd joined Dr. W. G. Grace as a member of the losing England XI in the Test Match of 1882 against Australia, following which the *Sporting Times* printed a mock obituary lamenting the death of English cricket, saying: 'The body will be burned and sent to Australia'. The following winter, in Australia, C. T. Studd again played, when England reversed the result. A group of ladies burned a cricket ball, sealing the remains in an urn before presenting them to the English captain Ivo Bligh (later Lord Darnley). Thus the Ashes were created (or is that cremated!) and brought back to England. In his will Lord Darnley bequeathed the urn to the M.C.C. who permanently display it in the Memorial Gallery at Lords. C. T. Studd played, in

11.   The 'set of Studds' – J. E. K., C. T. and G. B., captains of Cambridge University Cricket XI, 1882–4.

all, five times for England against Australia. A brilliant all-rounder, he twice scored 1,000 runs and took 100 wickets in a season. He is still regarded as one of cricketing's greats.

He firmly retained his commitment to religion however, even taking members of the England XI to hear D. L. Moody speak. Against his family's advice he arranged to go to China as a missionary, persuading six of his old university friends to join him on an extraordinary mission. The group, including a Dragoon Guardsman, an officer in the Royal Artillery and a famous university oarsman became known, amidst great national publicity, as the 'Cambridge Seven'. They toured Britain before leaving, spreading the evangelist gospel. At final meetings in Cambridge, Oxford and London, before crowded gatherings, they renounced their careers, wealth and social circles. C. T. Studd himself gave up a large fortune which he was due to inherit at the age of twenty-five. He gave away his inheritance to gospel charities, including £5,000 to Moody and a large donation to General Booth of the Salvation Army. In February 1885 they sailed for Shanghai where C. T. met his future wife, Priscilla Stewart, also a missionary. They married and moved inland to carry on their work, suffering much personal deprivation and at times being badly treated by the Chinese. They started an opium refuge for addicts, dealing with over 800 in seven years. C. T. and

Priscilla stayed in China for 10 years, absorbing themselves completely into the local culture. When they returned to England in 1894 their children spoke only Chinese and had to have an English tutor.

His gospel work continued and he spent 18 months on a preaching crusade in the U.S.A. Moving overseas once more, from 1900–6, C. T. ran the Union Church in Ootacumund, South India (Ooty), even joining a cricket tour in 1904 and making two double centuries! Back in England he still felt the call for overseas gospel work and in 1910 he sailed for Africa, running a mission in Khartoum, then travelling to Southern Sudan through malarial and sleeping-sickness infected country.

He next planned a crusade into the depths of the Belgian Congo, trekking for nine months through fever-ridden country and finally setting up a mission in the heart of Africa at Niangara in 1913. C. T.'s wife had stayed in England but was incredibly active in gospel work, organising a headquarters of world-wide missionary projects and travelling to the U.S.A., Canada, Australia, Tasmania, New Zealand, and South Africa. She was reportedly a fine, powerful speaker. C. T.'s brother George (G. B.) was also a missionary before becoming Principal of a theological college in California. The other member of the 'set', Kynaston (J. E. K.), was Lord Mayor of London from 1928–9. By the late '20s C. T. was weak, frail and frequently struck down by sickness. In 1928 Priscilla paid him a flying visit in Africa, staying just a fortnight. They were never to meet again. Priscilla died suddenly whilst on a visit to Spain in 1929. The following year C. T. was made 'Chevalier of the Royal Order of the Lion' by the King of the Belgians for services to the Congo. He died there on 16 July 1931, in the heart of Africa, his burial attended by about two thousand people who came to salute the passing of the grand old man.

'Like a Phoenix . . .'

Two years before the death of Edward Studd, in 1876, Francis Sloane Stanley put Tedworth House up for sale. It was bought by Sir John Kelk, a well-known civil engineer who moved to Tidworth after Studd's death, selling his estate at Bentley Priory, which was to be used during World War Two as the Headquarters of R.A.F. Fighter Command. Kelk was the leading building contractor in London, where he had been responsible for many landmark sites such as the Great Exhibition (1851), the Albert Memorial (1864), Millwall Docks (1868), Victoria Station (1858–60) and Smithfield Market (1866–9). With this background in building work it is not surprising that Sir John Kelk was to plan major alterations to Tedworth House, described later. From 1865–68 Sir John was Member of Parliament for Harwich. He was created 1st baronet in 1874 and in the following year became High Sheriff of Hampshire.

Since the demolition of the old South Tedworth church in 1784 only the small family chapel (now the Burial Chapel) had existed for worship in South Tedworth. Kelk arranged for the building of a new church, St Mary's, just a few hundred yards from Tedworth House, standing beside what is now the A338 close to the site of the original medieval church. His wife Rebecca Anne laid the foundation stone on 29 April 1879; this can still be clearly seen on the side of the church nearest the main road. A church of unusual design, with many 13th-century features, St Mary's was finished in 1880 and used as the South Tedworth village church until being closed and declared 'redundant' from 1 September 1972. It is maintained by the Redundant Churches Fund and remains consecrated. Occasional services and wedding ceremonies are still held there at the time of writing. More details of Tidworth's churches are given in Appendix I.

During the time he was awaiting occupancy of the house Sir John Kelk must have been carefully planning the extensive structural alterations which were to begin in 1878, soon after his arrival. Using the building contractors Messrs. Cubitt he brought in an 'army' of

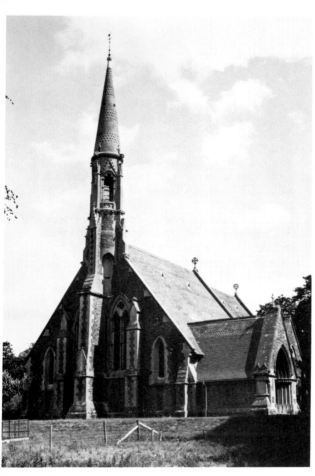

12. St Mary's church, South Tidworth, built for Sir John Kelk in 1880.

13. The monogram of Sir John Kelk below the clock tower, Tedworth House.

over 200 men who worked for two years to restructure the house, probably largely unchanged since Assheton Smith had ordered its rebuilding in 1830. A contemporary newspaper account describes the scene as 'an utter babel of sights and sounds as out of the ashes of the old mansion there is arising, phoenix-like, an imposing structure'. There were tramways, steam travelling cranes and workmen 'apparently on every square yard of the surface'. Massive stone columns and sculptured slabs of masonry lay everywhere in what to the uninitiated visitor seemed like total confusion. At the same time Kelk arranged for the planting of the avenue of lime trees which today, despite some storm damage, provide a magnificent wooded drive down to the house.

His most extensive work was on the south side of the house facing the well-kept lawns, flower gardens and Tedworth Park. He converted the old Georgian-looking south face with its bow-shaped centrepiece into a fine Palladian style with four inset giant Ionic columns, their bottom parts fluted, and each carrying a pediment. The three first-floor windows on the central portico were changed from rectangular to arched at the top and balconies added. Further stone balconies were put in place under the upper windows on either side with matching roof adornment. New facings of Portland stone were extensively added right around the building, together with ornate stonework around windows and the roof line.

Above the upper central windows on the south side a large sculptured coat of arms can be seen within a triangular pediment. The author has identified this as that of Sir John Kelk; it clearly displays his main symbol, three escallops. Beneath his coat of arms is his motto, 'Laetus sorte vives sapienter', which can be translated as: 'You will live wisely contented with your lot'. Kelk also installed the magnificent stained glass windows in the outer hall and central hall. All the stained glass seems to reflect Kelk's love of the country, each section containing scenes of birds, animals, insects and fish in their natural environment. The north-facing windows in both halls contain Kelk's coat of arms in full colour, the one in the central hall also including the Kelk crest: 'A wolf serjant erect sa. collared or, holding between the paws a leopard's face ppr, jessant-de-lis arg'. Quite a dramatic image.

In this same window is the inscription 'Ranae Regem A Jove Petentes', which may be translated as 'Frogs seeking a King from Jupiter'. Research by the author finally revealed this to relate to an Aesop's Fable concerning a group of frogs who prayed to the God Jupiter for a king to be appointed over them. Jupiter at first threw a log which created such a splash that the frogs kept a respectful distance. After a while they found their new monarch to be sluggish and dull, even boldly climbing on his back without a reaction, so they asked Jupiter for a more active king. This time Jupiter sent them a stork which quickly ate as many frogs as it could. They pleaded to Jupiter again but he pointed out that their plight was the result of not letting well alone. Both the log and the stork, as well as the frogs, appear on the window in a re-enactment of the fable. Looking down on the scene is the face of Jupiter himself (see Plate 14).

It appears that Sir John Kelk also had the carriage porch added to the north side of the building in front of the huge conservatory which extended from the corridor in the old service wing. Before the Portland stone carriage porch (porte-cochère) was built, the main entrance to the house was on the elaborately columned east side. Earlier drawings of the house show the four Ionic pillars standing out from the east face of the building, under a porch, to form an imposing main entrance. Today these pillars are 'boxed in' with Portland stone. Kelk therefore seems to have closed this entrance and incorporated it into what is now known as the ballroom, thus extending the room outwards, leaving what were external columns lying within the room. The first-floor bedrooms above the ballroom have also been extended over the old entrance.

Much work was obviously done at this time on the domed central hall or saloon with

14. The north window in the central saloon depicting a fable by Aesop.

15. *The Three Graces* from the central saloon.

16. Cottages in North Tidworth built by Sir John Kelk. Note the unusual slate fencing and horse hitching-post.

its walls running up through both floors. The grand staircase is framed by Tuscan columns, the stairs leading up to the master and best bedrooms above. At the top of the first flight of stairs is a sculpture of *The Three Graces* copied from the Canova original. Just when the sculpture was put in place is not known but it could well have been during the restructuring. *The Three Graces* are described in more detail in Appendix II.

After two years' work there had arisen a much more palatial mansion, looking like a new house with its white Portland facings and ornate masonry. Sir John was able to enjoy his refurbished house for several years until his death in 1886, when he was succeeded by his son Sir John William Kelk, 2nd bart. (1851–1923). John William Kelk had been born into the life of a country squire and took up the reins at Tedworth with ease. He built a number of houses in the village, some still standing, including the Reading Room and cottage by the junction of the Bulford Road with what is now Lahore Road, and a row of three brick and flint cottages still standing today about eighty yards east of the *Ram Inn*. His involvement is marked by the inscription 'J W K 1890' in stone on the front of the centre cottage.

A keen horseman, Kelk hunted and regularly attended race meetings at Stockbridge. He continued the tradition of 'lawn meets', gathering his pack in front of Tedworth House after breakfast, then mounting and heading off in search of a fox, often beginning the hunt in Assheton Coppice where the prey would lie sleeping. Even at this time the hunt would often sport more than 100 riders. John William Kelk was an officer in the Wilts. Yeoman Cavalry, holding the rank of Major. In 1892 he was appointed Sheriff of the County of Wiltshire. He took his estate duties seriously and was active in maintaining the welfare of his tenants. Soon, however, the Tedworth squirearchy was to come to an end, as part of the great changes which would profoundly affect life in this little border village. Kelk died in London at his home 40 Grosvenor Square on 23 March 1923, having been the last private owner of Tedworth House, which he had sold to the War Department in 1897.

Tidworth was to experience the same transformation, from small village to major military centre, which Aldershot had undergone in the 1850s. In 1853, following a military reconnaissance of potential training areas along the Hampshire/Surrey border, it had been decided to establish a large permanent barracks in Aldershot. Over 25,000 acres of land were purchased by the War Department and the following year construction of 'The Camp' began. Some indication of the rapid expansion of Aldershot can be seen from the massive rise in population from 875 in 1851 to 16,720 in 1861. News that the War Office was planning to build a similar military centre at Tidworth must have excited some villagers, who recognised enhanced business opportunities, but upset others as they realised that life in what were then the two 'model' villages of North and South Tidworth would never be the same again.

Part Three – The Military Take Over

Military Manoeuvres

In the latter half of the 19th century military exercises, or manoeuvres as they were usually called, were being mounted on an increasing scale, requiring extensive areas of open land. Manoeuvres had been held on Dartmoor, around Aldershot and occasionally on the Salisbury Plain but there was a lack of permanent fixed logistic facilities in these areas which were mostly privately owned and over which the military had no control. The need to regulate the use of land by the military had been recognised with the passing of the Military Lands Act 1892 which gave the Secretary of State for War new powers to purchase and lease land for military purposes. Salisbury Plain offered many attractive features as a training and exercise area as well as being well located in relation to Southampton, Aldershot and London. The chalk downland provided a firm well-drained surface for the passage of horses and heavy military transport, and it was a largely undeveloped area of little agricultural value with a low population.

The Government's intention to purchase 'a large tract of land for manoeuvering purposes on Salisbury Plain' was announced in the Commons by the Under Secretary of State for War on 29 January 1897. He asked for a sum of £450,000 to be authorised for 'urgent military purposes' to obtain this land which turned out to comprise about 40,000 acres of the plain, including Sir John William Kelk's Tedworth estate. To manage this enormous enterprise and deal with the problems of existing tenants' rights, estate management and military development, a body was formed in 1897 called the War Office Salisbury Plain Committee. The Committee, consisting of the Parliamentary Under Secretary of State, the Financial Secretary, the Adjutant General, the Quartermaster General and the Inspector General of Fortifications, met for five years, the last meeting being held on 25 April 1902.

Kelk had been interested in selling his estate since 1893 but had been unable to find a private buyer. When he was approached by the War Department he seems to have readily agreed to the sale which was finally completed on 29 September 1897. The estate consisted of 6,616 acres of land including Tedworth House itself, 13 farms, 8 farmhouses, 107 cottages, the observatory and the *Ram Inn*, North Tidworth. The War Department paid £95,000 for the whole estate which extended from North Tidworth to Shipton Bellinger in the south, east to Perham Down and included what is now the garrison area to the west. No obvious military function could be found for Tedworth House and other parts of the estate so, whilst the sale was being finalised in July 1897, it was proposed by the Salisbury Plain Committee that the house, together with the *Ram Inn*, some cottages and 2,200 acres of the estate, be put up for auction. This was arranged for 28 July 1897 but no buyer came forward, leading the committee to consider a private sale. Before this could be arranged, however, an intervention by the Adjutant General, Sir Redvers Buller V.C., G.C.B., G.C.M.G., led the committee to agree to try to find a tenant for Tedworth House.

In the meantime Sir John William Kelk, who was moving to his London home, had to dispose of most of the contents of the house. A huge sale, by auction, was arranged for five days in July 1897, with transport organised for buyers from Ludgershall station to Tedworth House ("at a moderate charge'). The Midland and South Western Junction Railway Company even arranged for the express train to stop at Ludgershall on the days of the sale to convey passengers to London, via Andover. The 64–page sale catalogue lists a staggering array of items from horses and carriages, valuable oil paintings, Louis XIV, Italian and Spanish furniture to pure-bred shorthorn Jersey cows! Even the most trifling items were advertised – 'two pairs kneecaps', 'two sets bandages', pots of jam, bedding, flower pots and Lot 181, 'Sinclair's Favourite Chemical Fire Extincteur, with shoulder straps and pedestal for same'. Kelk's 'Cellar of High Class Wines' came under Lots 1153 to 1260; Bins 1 to 88. Much of the wine appears to have been unsold as Sir John later asked the Salisbury Plain Committee if he could brick up the cellar until he could arrange to remove the contents. This was agreed! Also put up for sale, under Lot 292, was 'A Life Size Plaster Group of the Three Graces'. As this statue still stands today on the Grand Staircase it was presumably unsold, or bought and then presented back. A description of *The Three Graces* and further details of the sale of the house are given in Appendices II and III respectively. In all, 1,676 lots were put under the hammer between 12 and 16 July 1897.

In this same month the nation was to mark Queen Victoria's 60th year on the throne. The Tidworth jubilee celebrations, mainly paid for by Sir John, included a picnic tea for the village children in Savernake Forest and a sports meeting held at the base of Clarendon Hill with the Tedworth Band in attendance. All the men of North and South Tidworth and Shipton Bellinger were invited to dinner at Tedworth House; the women and children were given a special tea. The spectacular finale to the celebrations was a gathering of all the villagers and their children on Windmill Hill between Tidworth and Ludgershall. It was a special 'stay-up' occasion and at 9.30 p.m. a huge bonfire was lit by Mrs. Harrison, accompanied by Sir John, to mark the end of the jubilee celebrations. It burned long into the night consuming eight cartloads of wood, 4,000 faggots and 400 gallons of tar.

By early 1898 no tenant had been found for Tedworth House and the committee began to accept that the War Office itself would have to maintain it for a period. At a meeting held in October 1898 the committee decided to retain the house and its grounds. During a further meeting in December it was decided to hand over Tedworth House to the Commanding Royal Engineer, Salisbury Plain, Colonel R. M. Barklie who was supervising the construction of the new barracks at Tidworth. Colonel Barklie was able to use the house as personal quarters, accommodation for his staff and a central drawing office. In this drawing office many plans were produced for the massive building programme soon to be undertaken in Tidworth. Col. Barklie thus became the first military occupant of Tedworth House, holding the appointment of Comd. R.E. at Tidworth from 1898–1900.

The second military occupant of Tedworth House appears to have been Maj.-Gen. Thomas Arthur Cooke who held the appointment of General Officer Commanding Salisbury Plain from 5 May 1900 until 31 October of the same year. The Army Lists for Sept.-Oct. 1900 record Gen. Cooke's postal and telegraphic address as 'Tidworth House' so it seems that he had both his headquarters and residence at the house. Born on 20 January 1842, Gen. Cooke began his military service as an Ensign in the 5th Foot in 1862 before serving in the 17th Lancers from 1866 until his promotion to Acting Colonel in 1886. A veteran of the Zulu Campaign he fought in the Battle of Ulundi in 1879, where he was mentioned in despatches. He served in India from 1888 until 1899, finishing his overseas service as Brig.-Gen. India. Salisbury Plain was to be his last command, although he stayed on the active list for several more years.

As large numbers of labourers began to be recruited to build the new barracks in Tidworth accommodation had to be found for them and their families. A 'village' of corrugated iron shacks was put up for them in Brimstone Bottom, Ludgershall, which became known locally as 'Tin Town'. Navvy Village, to use its official title, even had its own iron church. The Midland & South Western Junction Railway (M.& S.W.J.R.) agreed to the construction of a branch line linking Tidworth to Ludgershall. Work began on the line in 1900, which opened the following year for military traffic. The major use of the line

HANTS AND WILTS.

PARTICULARS WITH PLAN

OF THE

TEDWORTH PARK ESTATE

A HIGHLY IMPORTANT

FREEHOLD RESIDENTIAL PROPERTY,

COMPRISING AN

Exceptionally Fine Mansion,

FINE WELL TIMBERED PARK & PLEASURE GROUNDS,

NUMEROUS COMPACT FARMS,

WITH EXCELLENT FARM HOUSES AND MODERN HOMESTEADS;

OVER 750 ACRES OF WOODLANDS & PLANTATIONS,

Forming fine Game Coverts, for which the Estate is noted; together with the

KENNELS OF THE WELL KNOWN TEDWORTH HOUNDS

The whole of the Villages of South and North Tedworth, and part of Shipton Bellinger,

FORMING ALTOGETHER A FINE

SPORTING AND RESIDENTIAL DOMAIN,

Extending over an area of

6,618 ACRES,

Situated in the Parishes of NORTH and SOUTH TEDWORTH and SHIPTON BELLINGER, 3 miles from Ludgershall
Station on the Andover and Swindon Branch, and 5 miles from Grateley on the Main Line of the South Western Railway,
whence ,London, which is 74 miles distant, is reached in 2 hours; about 15 miles north of Salisbury, and about the
same distance south of Marlborough.

FOR SALE BY PRIVATE CONTRACT

BY

Messrs. DANIEL SMITH, SON & OAKLEY.

Further Particulars and Plans may be obtained of Messrs. DANIEL SMITH, SON & OAKLEY, Land Agents,
Surveyors and Auctioneers, 10, Waterloo Place, Pall Mall, London, S.W., where Views of the Mansion and Park may

17.   Sale particulars for Tedworth House, 1897.

at this time was the transport of thousands of tons of building material for the construction of the new Tidworth Barracks. Although acting as a company branch line, it was always to remain under the control of the War Department. A siding was laid down to Brimstone Bottom allowing workmen to travel to Tidworth each day in open railway wagons on the 'Tin Town Mail'.

18.   Tidworth railway station, opened in 1902.

With the completion of the barracks many thousands of troops began to arrive in Tidworth by train along with thousands of tons of coal, rations and military stores to maintain the garrison. The regiments were able to use the train to 'export' a valuable resource – horse manure to feed the Hampshire strawberry beds and army dog droppings which went in barrels to tanneries in the Midlands. The railway station at Tidworth was in the peculiar position of lying directly on the county border. Passengers standing in the booking hall in Hampshire would pass their fare across to the booking clerk in Wiltshire!

So busy did traffic on the line become that Tidworth station was the senior one on the Midland & South Western, and the station-master's appointment was made the highest-ranking in the company. A military branch line into the barracks was built, crossing Pennings Road by bridge and then traversing the length of the garrison to finish at Aliwal Barracks in the west. Trains often needed assistance from other engines to climb back up the hill to the M.& S.W.J.R. line (which in 1923 became part of the Great Western Railway, then in 1948 the Western Region of British Railways).

The Generals Move In

Colonel R. M. Barklie continued to serve in Tidworth co-ordinating the barrack plans. He was made 'temporary' Brig.-Gen. on 28 January 1901 in command of Salisbury Plain District (Army List, April 1901), an appointment he held until his retirement on 30 January 1903 at the age of fifty-seven. He had been supervising military officer of the Tidworth garrison project for nearly five years and had no doubt hoped to see it through to completion but work, started by the contractors Henry Lovatt Ltd. of Wolverhampton in 1902, had fallen behind and the barracks would not be ready for occupation until 1904/5.

19.   The newly-constructed Tidworth barracks, c.1904.

An interesting feature of the new barracks was that the ground-plan of four infantry barracks at the centre and two cavalry barracks on each flank was modelled on the deployment of the Royalist and Parliamentary Armies in the Battle of Marston Moor (July 1644), the decisive engagement of the Civil War and the last great battle to have been fought on English soil. Named in alphabetical order after battles in India, the eight barracks were separated, as they are today, by roads mainly bearing the names of towns and villages in India and Afghanistan, recalling the days of Empire and the Raj. From west to east the barracks were named Aliwal, Assaye, Bhurtpore, Candahar, Delhi, Jellalabad, Lucknow and Mooltan. The roads themselves were also named alphabetically from west to east starting with Adampur Road and ending with Nainital Road. Later two more roads, Nepaul and Plassey, were built in the east of the garrison.

Whether Brig.-Gen. Barklie re-occupied Tedworth House after the departure of Maj.-Gen. T. A. Cooke is not known, as the next reference in the Army Lists is in 1904, as the address of Salisbury Plain District. Field Marshal Sir Evelyn Wood V.C., G.C.B., G.C.M.G., who at Salisbury commanded the 2nd Army Corps then Southern Command (1901–4), was offered the house as his residence but refused it on the grounds of cost. This decision displeased the War Office as they had retained it for this purpose. Southern Command Headquarters moved from Salisbury to Tidworth in 1905, apparently subsuming Salisbury Plain District. A famous soldier Lt.-Gen. Sir Ian Hamilton, K.C.B., D.S.O., was appointed General Officer Commanding-in-Chief, Southern Command, accepting Tedworth House as his official residence.

General Ian (Standish Monteith) Hamilton was a professional career soldier, articulate and charming with one of the keenest intellects in the army and a brilliant gift of expression. He was in the tradition of the British poet-generals, reading and writing poetry throughout his life. A slight, sensitive man, he walked with a limp due to a war injury which had left his left leg shorter than the other. The fingers of his left hand were also damaged, shrivelled by another war wound. A highly courageous officer, he had been recommended for the Victoria Cross no fewer than three times. Born on the island of Corfu on 16 January 1853, he was to live to a great age, surviving both World Wars. He had seen active service in the 2nd Afghan War, had transformed the use of musketry in the Indian army and was involved in the Gordon Relief Expedition. He served on the North West Frontier (1890–98) and then fought in the Boer War, being present at the Siege of Ladysmith. A favourite of Kitchener, Hamilton had been his Chief of Staff in 1901–2. In 1903 Hamilton became Quartermaster-General and in the following year he was appointed official British observer to the Russo-Japanese War in Manchuria.

Returning from Manchuria to take up his appointment as G.O.C. Southern Command at Tidworth, he spent the first summer in residence at Tedworth House working on what was to become the standard work on the Russo-Japanese conflict, *A Staff Officer's Scrap Book*, published in two volumes between 1905 and 1907. It was a controversial book, taking an independent line, which met with official disapproval in some quarters. When the second volume was ready in January 1906 Edward VII at first forbade its publication. When Hamilton met the King in Portsmouth at the launching of *H.M.S. Dreadnought* Edward is said to have wagged his finger at him and told him to be very, very careful. The Americans were keen to see its publication, however, and Hamilton even had a letter of support from President Theodore Roosevelt himself. A year after his 'ban' the King relented and allowed the second volume to go into print.

Gen. Sir Ian Hamilton was to remain as G.O.C. Southern Command until 1909. He was responsible for much of the early development of Salisbury Plain as a military training area. A hutted camp had been built in Bulford in 1903 and the main camp at Larkhill in 1906. Many other smaller camps sprung up around them to accommodate the growing numbers of troops training on the plain, including Tidworth Park Camp which was sited just to the south-east of Tedworth House, straddling the Shipton Bellinger road alongside Ashdown Copse and across to the south of the sewage works. At Tidworth Park Camp and at Tidworth Pennings Camp, just to the north of the village, boys from the public schools' Officer Training Corps attended their summer camps in great numbers (see Plate 20). During the military training season, between April and September, 20,000 troops were encamped in the immediate vicinity of Tidworth. Hamilton's command extended as far north as Worcester and Warwick and down to Portsmouth in the south. Visiting royalty, passing through Portsmouth, would often be entertained at Tedworth House and shown a military display in the park or on the plain.

The cost of maintaining a large country house with a constant round of entertaining was enormous. Hardly an evening or weekend was without a party or function. Fortunately, Lady Hamilton had private means in the form of a substantial annuity and was prepared

20.   Officer Training Corps encamped at Tidworth Pennings.

to use this to cover the cost of both private and official entertainment. During the Hamilton's stay at the house there were intermittent reports by themselves and visitors of ghostly drumming noises at night. No explanation other than 'water pipes' was forthcoming. These reports of strange noises and of unaccountable movement of objects have continued up to the present day, imaginations no doubt fired by tales of the original 'Demon Drummer of Tidworth'.

A new War Minister R. B. Haldane (later Viscount Haldane of Cloan), was appointed in December 1905 and became a frequent visitor to Tedworth House. Haldane was to be responsible for an extensive series of army reforms during his term in office which ended in 1912. Much discussion of these reforms, which included the formation of the Territorial Army in 1907, would have taken place during Haldane's visits to the house. Hamilton was in full agreement with the War Minister's radical views and he arranged for the first ever Territorial Army camp to be held on Salisbury Plain in 1908.

At this time there was little mechanisation in the army and with three cavalry barracks in Tidworth the horse became the dominant feature of the village. They were used to draw every conceivable type of wagon and carriage, to carry mounted troops on exercise and to take part in the many parades and ceremonial duties undertaken by each regiment. Mules were also used in great numbers as working animals. To maintain the animals in good health a large station veterinary hospital was built in the north-west corner of Aliwal Barracks, just below Seven Barrows. The whole garrison echoed to the sound of hoof-beats, the jingle of stirrup and bit and the distant bark of shouted orders to cavalrymen learning their first military horsemanship in the riding school. Mingling with this, from blacksmiths' shops, forges and workshops, came the ringing sound of striking hammers. Another sense

21. Sir Ian and Lady Hamilton at Tedworth House in 1905.

was awakened when approaching Kirkee Road where, opposite Jellalabad Barracks, the garrison bakery was in operation. The appetising smell of freshly baked bread was a special characteristic of that part of the garrison. Next to the bakery was the butchery which arranged the military meat supply. Both buildings were still standing in 1991, the former being a riding stables known as the Bakery Stables.

Before World War I put the army into khaki most of the troops wore brightly coloured tunics or blue patrols and elaborate headwear, adding to the glamour of what was, after Aldershot, the second largest military garrison in Britain. On Sundays there was the unforgettable sight of each regiment leaving barracks to march with its military band to attend Church Parade. Clad in best uniform and plumed helmets, sunlight flashing on polished steel and brass, it must have been a stirring spectacle. Beginning in the west at Aliwal Barracks, bands playing at their head, each regiment marched along Grand Trunk Road to the garrison church, being successively followed by other regiments as they passed their respective barracks. In the east the resident regiment at Mooltan Barracks led in the parade from the other side of the garrison. Crowds would gather on both sides of the road, coming from as far as Salisbury, to watch the Sunday morning parades. One year was particularly memorable, with no less than three Regimental mascots on parade at the same time – the Argyles with their pony, the Welch with their goat and the Royal Warwicks with their antelope.

With the increasing troop numbers in Tidworth there was an urgent need for welfare and recreational facilities. To this end a large welfare centre named (after the General) the Ian Hamilton Wesleyan Soldiers' Home was built, opening on 4 July 1908. Mr. R. B. Haldane the War Minister was present at the opening, together with Sir Ian and Lady Hamilton and Brig.-Gen. Sir Hubert Hamilton C.B., D.S.O. (no relation) who commanded 7 Infantry Brigade. The facilities included games rooms, a reading and writing room, a refreshment area, a concert room and a lecture hall. The impressive building still stands today at the junction of Bulford Road and Kohat Road, being used at the time of writing as a youth centre. Church accommodation was quite inadequate for the massively increased population. In the summer months services for troops were held in the grounds of Tedworth House to relieve pressure on the village churches, which had to hold staggered church parades on a Sunday for the troops. The first church to be built in the garrison was St Andrew's Presbyterian church, which opened for worship in January 1909. A larger building was required, however, to meet the needs of the soldiers and their families so proposals were put forward in 1907 for the building of a garrison church. With much backing from the Bishop of Salisbury and following a fund-raising campaign the Church of England garrison church of St Michael was finally completed in 1912. Further details of Tidworth's churches are given in Appendix I. The education of army children was organised by the War Department until 1948. When the army moved into Tidworth only one school existed in the village – Mrs. Assheton Smith's building dating back to 1857. As the garrison became established it became necessary to add new facilities, the first being the Tidworth Army School, a brick-built junior school constructed in 1909 in Bazaar Road just opposite the Garrison Theatre; a wooden senior school was built just behind it. Both schools were still in use in 1991, as an infants' and junior school.

In 1909 Hamilton left Tidworth to take up the appointment of Adjutant-General, and then served as G.O.C. Mediterranean & Inspector General of Overseas Forces. At the outbreak of the First World War he was unexpectedly called in by Kitchener to command the Central Force in England. The Great War, however, was to sour the reputation of an outstanding soldier in the twilight of his career. Kitchener sent Hamilton to command the military forces, numbering 75,000, involved in the naval assault on the Gallipoli Peninsula in Turkey. From his headquarters, largely ship-board in the Dardanelles Straits, General Hamilton was involved in a complex, stressful campaign which resulted in massive losses of men. His judgement was finally called into question and he was relieved of his command. He was never to be given another. The events at Gallipoli came to be regarded as a débâcle, with much criticism being levelled at those in high command both on the ground and back in Britain.

General Sir Ian Hamilton, G.C.B., G.C.M.G., D.S.O., was to spend the rest of his long life obsessed with restoring his reputation. In 1920 he published *Gallipoli Diary* in which he explained the campaign from his perspective, but cold historical analysis was unrelenting and his earlier reputation as a soldier of distinction was never fully recovered. He took up the prestigious position of Lieutenant of the Tower of London in 1918 and was made Rector of Edinburgh University in 1932. Living to see the whole of the Second World War, he passed away in London on 12 October 1947 at the age of ninety-four.

His successor General Sir Charles Douglas G.C.B. (1850–1914), another distinguished soldier, also used Tedworth House as his private residence. Joining the 92nd Highlanders in 1869, he had taken part in the Afghan War (1879–80) where he was involved in many actions, including the march from Kabul for the relief of Kandahar where his horse was shot from beneath him and he was twice mentioned in despatches. He had been in the Transvaal Campaign during the South African War in 1881 and was again mentioned in despatches during the Sudan Campaign in 1885. Back in Africa for the Boer War (1899–1901) he commanded the 9th Infantry Brigade and later a column, taking part in many operations and being mentioned in despatches again in 1901. He was promoted to Major-General for distinguished service and awarded the Queen's Medal with four clasps. On returning to England he held several commands before being appointed Adjutant General 1904–09. He was to remain at Tedworth House from 1909 to 1912 as General Officer Commanding-in-Chief Southern Command. His portrait hangs on the wall of the present Tedworth House Officers' Mess in the central saloon.

General Sir Charles Douglas was to be the last person to use Tedworth House as a private residence. He left to become Inspector-General, Home Forces 1912–14, and had just been appointed A.D.C. General to the king in 1914 when he suddenly died on 25 October just after the outbreak of World War I. As General Douglas left Tedworth House, work was just being completed on four senior officers' residences a few hundred yards from the house in Arcot Road at the edge of Tidworth Park. These fine buildings,

22.   The central saloon, Tedworth House. The painting on the right is a mid 19th-century view of Tedworth hunt.

Clive, Havelock, Muir and Hastings House, are still in use today as senior officers' quarters. In the grounds of the house are two dogs' graves. Lying side by side, just outside one of the tennis courts to the south, the stones are inscribed as follows:

Smudge
Loving
Joyous Friend
Killed By
Motor
Jan 1917

Peter
Bull Terrier
Died 28 Sept 1904
Aged 7½

The Club Opens

At the beginning of the Great War Tedworth House changed its role to become an Officers' Club. A contemporary notice dated 5 April 1915 calls for officers to append their name if interested in joining the club. Subscription for a battalion was '£4 *per mensem*' (each month) which would work out at about two shillings per officer. Facilities included 'Golf Links and games generally'. This function continued into the 1920s although by 1929 Tedworth House was also used to accommodate nursing staff from the Tidworth Military Hospital which had been established at Delhi Barracks since 1907. During World War I Salisbury Plain became a major training area and transit centre for troops. Additional hutted camps to accommodate the vastly increased numbers of men were built at Larkhill, Bulford and Tidworth, that at Larkhill being the largest. Overseas troops moved into the garrison and a Canadian training depot was established at Tidworth as early as January 1915. The headquarters of the Australian Imperial Force Depots in the United Kingdom was set up in Bhurtpore Barracks in 1917, whilst in Candahar Barracks there were several other Australian army units. New Zealand troops were also on the plain in some numbers, many having been evacuated from Gallipoli.

Commonwealth graves in Tidworth cemetery are perhaps the only reminder today of their presence during World War I. Most of the 159 Australians and 100 New Zealanders buried here died in either the Tidworth or Fargo Military Hospitals, the latter being located on the Rollestone side of Larkhill. Some of the flavour of life of a British soldier in Tidworth during World War I may be gained from a poem, available as a printed postcard in 1916:

TIDWORTH

There's a certain place called Tidworth,
In the wilds of Salisbury Plain,
If I could only but escape
I'd ne'er go back again.

The place is noted far and wide,
A depot for Recruits, Trench Digging and Route Marches,
Which wears out all your boots!

The Scenery is beautiful,
You should see 'nine-tree hill',
Where we go through a performance,
Which the Poets call 'Swedish Drill'.

We rise each morn and half-past-five,
Just when Reveille blows,
And practice rapid-marching,
In charge of N.C.O.s.

Sometimes we go shooting,
To try and earn our Bounties,
But some of the shots I fired myself,
Could be found in several counties.

Tidworth's all right in its place,
With its valleys, and its dells;
But I would rather be in France,
Or else the Dardanelles.

To find a place like Tidworth,
Many miles you'd have to roam;
But I wish the war was over,
And I was back at home!

JIMMY W.

Although the 2nd Cavalry Brigade had distinguished themselves at Flanders, trench warfare in France had allowed no freedom for traditional cavalry action and when the tank began to appear on the battlefield in 1916 the days of the mounted assault were numbered. It was becoming apparent that the only place for the horse in war was as a transport animal. Plans were formulated to replace horses with motorised vehicles. With the end of the Great War conditions began to return to their former peacetime state, the two major formations at Tidworth in 1922 being the 2nd Cavalry Brigade and the 7th Infantry Brigade, the same as in 1914. The 7th Infantry Brigade was made up of four regiments, and the Cavalry Brigade was comprised of three regiments and about one thousand two hundred horses. The horse still reigned supreme and post-war mechanisation was slowed by continuing resistance from senior cavalry officers who, largely through sentiment, argued for the retention of the mounted trooper. Even after World War One the cavalryman still carried a lance, sword and rifle. Incidentally, the rank of 'trooper' only replaced 'private' in the cavalry of the line in 1923. Fundamental changes were not far off, however, and in 1928, as a result of progressive mechanisation, the first two cavalry regiments had their horses replaced by vehicles, mainly 7 h.p. Austin armoured cars.

Amalgamations of cavalry units were ordered in 1922, 18 regiments being halved to just nine. These amalgamations led to the formation of such units as the 17th/21st Lancers who served in Tidworth at Aliwal Barracks as part of the 2nd Cavalry Brigade from 1922 to 1925. The Commanding Officer of the 17th/21st Lancers Lt. Col. B. D. (Bertie) Fisher began the first of his landscaping projects in Tidworth with the building of a new football ground at Aliwal Barracks. Other regiments began to follow Fisher's example, each laying out football and cricket grounds in their unit lines to enhance greatly the recreational facilities in the garrison. Many of these sports fields still exist. By 1923 work on the sports fields was complete but Fisher had his eye on a bigger project, shortly to be described. He left his regimental command on promotion in 1923 to take over the Tidworth Cavalry Brigade. 'Bertie' Fisher was to have a bright military career, finishing his service as General Officer Commanding Southern Command in the rank of Lieutenant General.

A spectacular cavalry event occurred in 1925 when the 17th/21st Lancers packed and moved to Aldershot. Following a breakfast with the 14th/20th Hussars and the Lancashire Fusiliers, the whole regiment moved off through Tidworth in mounted sections led by the Commanding Officer on a grey horse. With lance-flags fluttering, lance points glinting in the sun and all officers with swords drawn, it must have been a fine sight. Crowds gathered as the bands of the 12th Lancers and 14th/20th Hussars led the parade through the village, escorted by several troops of the 12th Lancers. Every band in the garrison played them out of Tidworth. On reaching Perham Down the accompanying bands and troops pulled away with a final cheer, leaving the regiment to travel by road via Basingstoke to their new home in Warburg Barracks, Aldershot.

The Garrison Theatre, standing at the junction of Bazaar Road and Lowa Road was one of the earliest places of recreation built for the troops, opening in 1909. Originally gas-lit, it was to stage every kind of entertainment from boxing tournaments, regimental dinners and military band concerts to full-scale variety shows, pantomimes, films and lectures. Many leading entertainers of the day, including Will Hay, Harry Champion, Norman Wisdom, and Eric Sykes have appeared on stage at the theatre. In 1926 the famous Australian Opera star Dame Nellie Melba G.B.E. gave her last performance in Britain at the theatre before returning home. During World War Two many productions were staged by E.N.S.A. bringing many well known stars and budding hopefuls to the garrison. Bob Hope and James Cagney were two of the many famous overseas stars to entertain the troops. Military lectures and briefings by prominent generals such as Wavell, Montgomery and Eisenhower have been held in the theatre both during and after both World Wars.

23.   The Electric cinema, Kirkee Road.

The building today is exceptionally well-preserved, still having the original pitch-pine floor from 1909, over which millions of soldiers' feet have pounded. It is one of the very few, if not the only, garrison theatres of that vintage still in existence in the country. Another remarkable facet of the Garrison Theatre story is the involvement of the Pickernell family – firstly Bert Pickernell who came from the Swindon Empire, to whom it was leased, as stage manager in 1909 then ran it up to his retirement in 1946. His son Ken took up the reins, running it until 1987 when his son Tony took over to carry on the family tradition; he was still manager in 1991.

Recreational facilities for the troops were further improved with the opening of new welfare centres and cinemas – the Electric cinema in Kirkee Road, which began full operation in 1913 with the opening of the power station, and the Hippodrome cinema, seating 612 people, probably built during World War One. As well as providing entertainment for the troops the Electric cinema had Saturday morning shows for children, with piano accompaniment in the days of silent movies. The admission charge in the 1920s was just one penny. Later in its life the Electric cinema became rather shabby, deserving its local nickname 'The Flea-Pit'. Its image was not helped by a notorious manager, Mr. Locke, who frequently appeared front of house in a vest and was known to stop a film in the middle to direct a tirade at the troops for their behaviour. On one occasion when a film failed to start he was found in the projection box lying amongst reels of celluloid somewhat the worse for wear! The much larger Hippodrome cinema was situated in Pennings Road between what is now a garage and the Royal British Legion Club; the cinema burnt down in 1963. The Royal British Legion has a long history in the village, the first club being built in 1922 only a year after the formation of the British Legion itself. It was replaced by the existing building, put up on the same site, in 1962.

Below the railway station, on what is now Station Road, shops and other services had become established. Known to the troops in the 1920s as 'Robbery Row' the shops nevertheless provided 'High Street' facilities in the village and were a valued asset in such a remote location. Two of the existing shops – Dickinson's and Semple's – are shown on a street map of 1918 together with The Capital & Counties Bank (now Lloyd's Bank). The Lloyd's Bank building, erected about 1915, is an early example of the work of Sir Edward Maufe. Today Station Road is still the bustling centre of village activity, providing a good range of shops for both the military and civilian population.

Within the barrack area itself the Tidworth garrison market had sprung up, more commonly known as the 'Tin Market' due to its corrugated iron construction. It stood, until the 1950s, on a site which is now the car park of the Garrison Theatre. About twenty stalls operated, under the control of the Garrison Adjutant, providing greengrocers, butchers, grocers, a fishmonger, a chemist, a tobacconist and outfitter's amongst others. Troops also shopped at the Navy, Army and Air Force Institute (N.A.A.F.I.) establishments which opened at Tidworth, Bulford and Larkhill following the formation of the organisation in 1921. N.A.A.F.I. also provided canteen facilities to the many tented camps across the Salisbury Plain.

There was some excitement in the village when, in April 1920, the extraordinary Percy Toplis – an army deserter, First World War mutineer, confidence trickster and anti-hero (recently brought to public notice by the B.B.C. television drama *The Monocled Mutineer* and a book of the same name) – was the subject of a murder hunt, having allegedly shot a Salisbury taxi-driver, Sidney Spicer, at Thruxton Down just outside Tidworth. He escaped in Spicer's grey Darracq taxi, driving through Tidworth, finally abandoning the vehicle in Wales. The Hampshire police set up what was to become the most intensive manhunt ever mounted, with dramatic newspaper coverage following Toplis' exploits as he popped up to taunt the police right across the country, then slipped into hiding again. He was reported in no less than 107 locations and there were several false arrests. It resulted in a tragic end for a cavalryman stationed in Tidworth. Private Coop of the 9th Lancers, awaiting trial for desertion in the unit guardroom at Tidworth, escaped and headed east into the countryside. A few miles away at Collingbourne he stopped at a cottage to ask for help but was mistaken for Percy Toplis and chased away. Stealing a bicycle, he headed for Burbage by which time local people were on his tail. He beat them off but could not evade police following in a car. He was then picked up by the regimental police, escaped again, and was once again arrested by police and taken back to his unit. A short time later Private Coop was found dead in his guardroom cell having hanged himself with a strip of clothing. Toplis headed for Scotland where, in a confrontation in a remote Highland village, he shot and wounded a policeman and a gamekeeper, evading capture. He took a train down into Cumberland and was recognised in Penrith where he was caught in a police ambush, dying in a hail of bullets.

In this same year the *Ram Inn*, North Tidworth, finally reverted to private ownership, being purchased by the Portsmouth United Breweries on 28 January 1920. It had been bought by the War Department as part of Sir John William Kelk's Tedworth estate in 1897 and had remained under W.D. control ever since. The *Ram Inn*, rebuilt since the 1920s, still acts as the main village 'local'. Off-duty life for soldiers in such an isolated garrison could, however, be very dull in the 1920s. After the First World War the public had no stomach for war and the army was held in fairly low esteem. Officers hunted, played polo and cricket and could usually get away at weekends in their new passport to

24.   The *Ram*, North Tidworth, *c.*1920.

freedom – the motor car. One cavalry officer is remembered for flying in and out each weekend in his red biplane! Cavalry officers also arranged for the construction of a race-course at nearby Windmill Hill where regimental races were held and for five days each year horse-racing under National Hunt Rules was allowed. As a cavalry station, Tidworth was regarded by many officers as having no equal in the United Kingdom.

The Tidworth Tattoo also dates from this time, being held for the first time from 8–10 June 1920. This event was to grow from a small 'pageant' performance for the troops and a few local residents to a nationally-known military display attracting audiences of 150,000. It was even advertised in France on specially produced handbills. The early tattoos were held on the polo field in front of the south side of Tedworth House, lit by searchlights mounted on the roof of the house. The 'control tower' consisted of two barrack-room tables behind a screen with a portable telephone connecting it to the light operators on the roof. After 1925 the tattoos moved a little further to the southern end of Tidworth Park, on to what is now the arena site, where a natural amphitheatre is formed. Becoming ever more professional, the tattoo was held in early summer for the next 18 years, only stopping when preparations for war led to the cancellation of the 1939 event. It was to be 27 years before the next tattoo was mounted, and this 1966 display was held in daylight without the drama of searchlights stabbing the darkness. At its peak the tattoo ran for seven evenings, floodlit by searchlights generating over 700 million candle-power, the performance lasting two-and-a-half hours from dusk to midnight.

As the event developed it became necessary to improve the facilities for the growing audiences. Electric cables and telephone lines were buried beneath an area specially turfed, mainly by the military. Local troops dug out and transported over 20,000 skip loads of earth and cut 100,000 pieces of turf from Perham Down to prepare the arena. Seating was provided to replace the temporary stand which had stood at the bottom of the Tedworth House garden, leading eventually to the building of a covered stand with a royal box. This Tattoo Stand still exists, being used for horse shows and other displays. Profits from the early displays helped to improve and expand sports grounds and facilities in the garrison as well as aiding charities. The Tidworth Tattoo programme traditionally included displays of drill, physical training, motor cyclists, massed bands and fireworks as well as the famous torchlight display, performed to a backdrop of thousands of glowing red points of light as the audience drew on their cigarettes! Later displays included parachuting, mock battles and helicopter displays. At its height the Massed Bands display involved 16 regimental bands, numbering 1,000 men, who marched into the natural amphitheatre in full dress with pomp and precision. For weeks before the event took place uniform and costume-fitting sessions for soldiers took place in the Garrison Theatre. Further details of the Tidworth Tattoo can be found in N. D. G. James' book *Plain Soldiering* (*see* Bibliography). As military commitments grew, the resurrected tattoos could only be sustained for 10 years, the last event being held from 29–31 May 1976.

Tidworth Park is also known for the Fisher Polo Ground, named after Colonel B. D. Fisher who was in command of the 2nd Cavalry Brigade (1923–27). He was responsible for the organisation of the tattoo at that time and he arranged for a polo field to be laid by soldiers of his brigade during the landscaping of the new arena. It was completed in 1925. A memorial stone listing the units involved in the work today stands in tribute outside the club-house of the Tidworth Polo Club. Before this field was laid an earlier one, known as No. 1 Ground, was used. This had its own small pavilion and was located opposite St Mary's church, by the side of the A338, where a sports field now stands. Additional polo grounds were laid out in Tidworth during the 1930s at Perham Down and Tidworth Pennings just to the north of the village. The Fisher Ground helped Tidworth to achieve a premier position in polo circles, at one time being rated as second only to Hurlingham. Polo is still regularly played in Tidworth Park on the ground between Arcot Road and the River Bourne. Successive cavalry regiments have maintained the Tidworth Polo Club and are honoured with the continuing support of the royal family. Following in the footsteps of his father H.R.H. the Duke of Edinburgh, who played many times on the Fisher Ground, H.R.H. The Prince of Wales has competed regularly at Tidworth through-out his polo-playing career.

During the 1930s Tidworth established its position as one of the great military garrisons, well-ordered, not a blade of grass out of place, as much a model of its kind as the villages of North and South Tidworth had been before the arrival of the army. Up to the outbreak of the Second World War, Tedworth House continued to be used mainly as an Officers' Club. So established did it become that the road linking the house northwards with Humber Lane was named Club Lane. It is still signed as such today. Barracks were built at Perham Down in 1937 with the Matthew Barracks at Tidworth being added in 1939. As preparations for war continued there was an influx of British troops to the garrison making it once again a busy centre of military activity. No Commonwealth troops were based in Tidworth during World War Two, unlike World War One, but a new dimension was added to life in the village with the arrival of the Americans in 1942.

25. The coat of arms of Sir John Kelk within the central pediment on the south side of Tedworth House.

The War and After

The Headquarters of the U.S. II Corps was established at Tidworth under the command of General Mark Clark. Brig. Theodore ('Teddy') Roosevelt Jr., assistant commander of the U.S. 1st Infantry Division, had left the United States with 1,500 men in June 1942 and on arrival in England had joined the 16,000 or so other members of the division before being directed to Tidworth where they arrived on 8 August as the first U.S. unit. Seven other Armoured and Infantry Divisions of U.S. troops were to follow in the next two years, staying for variable periods. They took over almost the whole garrison, including some of the married quarters and the school in Bazaar Road.

Brig. 'Teddy' Roosevelt Jr. (1887–1944) was the eldest son of Theodore Roosevelt (1858–1919), the 26th President of the United States. Already a highly decorated soldier from World War One, Brig. Roosevelt was to play a significant role in the D-Day landings. His wife Eleanor, aged 53, who had applied for overseas volunteer service with the American Red Cross, was sent to England, arriving in September 1942. The American Adjutant General suggested she join her husband in Tidworth where, with 20,000 men but few recreational facilities, a Red Cross Club was badly needed. At Tidworth she was surprised to be offered Tedworth House for use as a soldiers' club by the local British Commander Maj.-Gen. Packenham Walsh. The house at that time was empty but for a small detachment of Royal Army Medical Corps soldiers who were occupying the kitchen and some staff quarters.

The Tidworth Military Hospital was being used as an American hospital and whilst quarters were being prepared at Tedworth House Eleanor Roosevelt lived in the hospital for a few days. She arrived at a time when 90 Voluntary Aid Detachment (V.A.D.) girls were being transferred from the hospital. Mrs. Roosevelt got permission from the War Office to use eight of the V.A.D. girls as workers in the Red Cross Club. She quickly mobilised a staff, including villagers, to set up a canteen for the U.S. troops. Working in what for the numbers involved were primitive conditions, they began cooking over 30 dozen hamburgers a night in two small frying pans and making over 80 gallons of coffee. Dishes were washed in fire buckets. It soon became established as a valued recreational facility, the amenities including a library, pianos, billiards, ping-pong, sitting rooms, hot showers, a barber's and a tailor. The troops poured in, one visitor remarking to Mrs. Roosevelt that it was 'Just wonderful. Like a cross between Bedlam and the Ritz'! One day, following the visit of a chimney sweep to the house, Mrs. Roosevelt found black sooty fingermarks in compromising places on the nude statues of *The Three Graces*. As she approached she heard a corporal shout, 'Get a rag and wash them dames off'!

A most active manageress, Eleanor Roosevelt proposed that the indoor tennis court, still in use today, be used to show films and theatrical performances. However, as the court had a glass roof there was a problem with blackout as a protection against enemy bombing. Not to be discouraged, she organised a work party to paint the glass black and shortly afterwards the first performance was held with an audience of 1,400 packed around the newly constructed stage to watch a show by a visiting U.S.O. troupe. Not long after this Bebe Daniels, a famous entertainer, brought her company to perform at Tedworth House. Six months after opening as a Red Cross Club a Jackson coffee boiler, a large hamburger grill and a doughnut machine were installed!

Each week a dance was held at the house with invitations sent to A.T.S. and W.A.A.F.s who came in uniform. W.R.E.N.s and Land Army girls were also invited to partner the troops. Other girls were transported from surrounding villages by the U.S. Motor Pool. It is said that the wartime dance the 'Hokey-Cokey' started at Tedworth House in 1943 before becoming 'the rage'. Certainly the first mention of the dance was in the *Dancing Times* of that year, but its true origin remains a mystery. The first winter after the Americans' arrival Tidworth was a sea of mud as jeeps and trucks tore around the village churning up the ill-prepared roads. The British were mortified at the appearance of the once immaculate 'model' British garrison.

The Red Cross Club at Tedworth House fulfilled a vital role in providing a warm place of recreation and entertainment for the many thousands of U.S. troops in the village. It was to remain there until the end of the war. June 1944 was a period of frantic activity as the Americans prepared to pull out of Tidworth to join other forces for the D-Day landings. The roads became choked with military vehicles heading for Southampton. Brig. Gen. Roosevelt was assistant divisional commander in the first wave of the Normandy landings. He was awarded the Medal of Honour for gallantry displayed in his leadership under fire.

The American integration into the village is well illustrated in the parish registers for 1944–5 which record whole batches of marriages of U.S. soldiers and officers to local girls. The last American troops left Tidworth in April 1946, allowing the Garrison to be run once again by the British. Even after the U.S. troops pulled out the American connection with the village was not quite finished. After the war Tidworth was appointed as an assembly point for 'G.I. brides' before they travelled to the U.S.A. to join their husbands. They were allocated transit camp accommodation at Jellalabad and Delhi Barracks in Tidworth as well as at Perham Down. In all, 640 women, their average age 23, arrived at Tidworth in a special train, bringing with them 176 babies. They were packed into the camp having to sleep four to a room. German prisoners of war at the camps were assigned

26. Wall plaque outside Tidworth garrison headquarters marking the U.S. army presence during World War Two.

as batmen to the transitees. The departure of the G.I. brides was to signal the end of the American involvement with the village, although some still return for a nostalgic visit.

During the Second World War two small military engines, *Betty* and *Molly*, became a familiar sight and were held in great affection by the troops as they worked the military line through the garrison. Following post-war demobilisation large parts of the garrison stood empty, much of it becoming vandalised and derelict. In the early '50s modernisation of some of the barracks was undertaken together with a married quarters building programme, although most of the existing married quarters date from the 1960s. The Ludgershall-Tidworth railway line closed to passenger traffic in 1955, a victim of the competition of road transport. Troop trains stopped in 1963 after which the line was pulled up and the station demolished. The present N.A.A.F.I. supermarket at the top of Station Road now stands where the station disgorged its thousands of passengers for over 60 years.

Following the Hungarian uprising in 1956, which was heavily suppressed by Russian troops, hundreds of Hungarian refugees were staged through Tidworth. They were processed in Mooltan Barracks and given clothing by the W.V.S. and other voluntary organisations before being sent on to more permanent homes. In 1967 the Globe cinema was opened just opposite the Station Road N.A.A.F.I.; it later became a bowling alley. During the 1950s Tedworth House once again became an Officers' Club whilst continuing to provide accommodation for sisters of Queen Alexandra's Royal Army Nursing Corps. For

27.   The north carriage porch, archway and clock tower, Tedworth House.

ease of referral, brief details of significant personalities and events in Tidworth from 1650 to the present day are given in Chronology Two.

Now a Mess

The Officers' Club finally ceased trading in September 1978, in part a victim of the soaring inflation of the period. The General Officer Commanding South West District gave authority for it to become a military Officers' Mess. Tedworth House became the Officers' Mess for 8 Field Force, which had been formed in 1977. During its time at Tidworth 8 Field Force's most notable achievement was to provide the leadership of the organisation which supervised the ceasefire in Rhodesia from December 1979 to March 1980. 8 Field Force moved to Aldershot in December 1981, and was re-titled 5 Infantry Brigade on 1 January 1982. At the same time 6 Field Force was re-titled 1st Infantry Brigade on its move from Aldershot to Tidworth. At the time of writing Tedworth House is still the Officers' Mess for 1st Infantry Brigade. Officers from other minor units, without a parent mess, are also members.

It was closed in 1982 for a major refurbishment which restored the house to some of its former elegance. During the closure of the mess resident officers were moved to the Candahar Officers' Mess. A re-opening cocktail party was held at Tedworth House on 8 July 1983 attended by Field Marshal Sir Edwin and Lady Bramall, who at that time were using Muir House in Tidworth Park as their country residence. The General Officer

Commanding South West District, Major General M. S. Gray O.B.E., also attended as a guest of the Tidworth Brigade Commander Brigadier (later the Hon.) W. E. Rous. To mark the event Mrs. Rous planted a tree on the grassed area in front of the carriage porch.

The old oak-panelled dining room has undergone several changes of name. When the house was an Officer's Club in the '60s the room was known as the red room, possibly because of the dark red fireplace. When the large gilded bar was installed in the '70s the room was called the gold bar. During the refurbishment of the mess in 1982–3 the gilded bar was removed and it was decided to name the room the library, presumably in ignorance of the fact that the original library had been in the green room opposite. Tedworth House was given Grade II listed building status in December 1986. The stable block, the indoor tennis court and the pair of gates leading off Stables Road into the kitchen garden were included in the listing. Grade II properties are 'Buildings of special interest which warrant every effort being made to preserve them'. To achieve Grade I listed status buildings must be of 'exceptional interest'; only about four per cent of listed buildings meet this criterion.

During the so-called 'Great Storm' of October 1987 considerable damage was done to trees in the village, including several of Kelk's beautiful lime trees in the avenue leading down to the house. Further, even more destructive storms in January and February 1990 brought down others in the avenue and throughout Tidworth Park. Fortunately most of the limes have survived and the avenue remains largely intact, the gaps being filled with new plantings. Actual structural damage occurred to the house when a large ornate chimney on the east side roof was struck by a 'thunderbolt' during a severe storm in May 1989. The whole chimney was split from its base, bringing huge chunks of masonry crashing through the roof into an officer's bedroom below. Luckily he was not in the room as the falling stonework smashed through his bed and wardrobe before creating a gaping hole in the floor.

Today the house looks much as it did following Sir John Kelk's late 19th-century refurbishment. Tennis courts have been added on the south side and a less welcome but necessary recent addition has been a perimeter security fence. The old conservatory windows have been bricked up and the palm house dismantled except for the floor and steps. On the lawn where the hunt used to assemble all that now disturbs the rabbits and birds on a summer's evening is the sound of croquet mallet and tennis racquet on ball.

The villages of North and South Tidworth continue to support a predominantly military population, forming one of the country's leading garrisons. On a walk round the garrison today the barrack and road names – Lucknow, Candahar, Jellalabad, Bazaar and so on – continue to evoke echoes of Empire India and those heady days of the British Raj. Almost unchanged externally since their building, the red and yellow brick barrack blocks present the eye with a grim but evocative image of their Edwardian origin. Changes are, however, in train with a major reconstruction of the barracks beginning as this book is being prepared. Starting with the demolition of Aliwal Barracks in the west of the garrison, there is to be a rolling exercise of rebuilding, each barracks being replaced by new buildings. This will take many years – probably decades – and it is hoped sufficient of the old will be preserved for us to continue to be taken back to the time of a pre-mechanised army, when over 1,000 cavalry horses were stabled in the famous garrison.

Major change is also afoot in the villages of North and South Tidworth themselves. As this book goes to print preparations are being made to change the Hampshire/Wiltshire boundary line which runs through the two villages. This change will bring the two villages into the same county – Wiltshire. No longer will they have separate police forces, schools, dustbin collections and local authorities; all is to be harmonised and simplified under a single county body. Many anomalies will be removed but at the same time, perhaps, Tidworth will have lost a little of its unique character.

Chronology Two – Tedworth House

This chronology covers the period from 1650 to the present day. It details significant events which took place in and around Tedworth House.

1650	Thomas Smith bought Tedworth House from Jane Ashburnham.
1661–2	The 'Drummer' poltergeist disturbances occurred in Tidworth.
1689	Tidworth Zouch almshouses built. Conveyed to John Smith of Tedworth House in 1691.
1699	John Smith made Chancellor of the Exchequer.
1705	John Smith appointed Speaker of the English Parliament.
1707	Act of Union between England and Scotland. John Smith first Speaker of British Parliament.
1784	South Tedworth church demolished. Stone used to build Burial Chapel in Church Lane.
1826	Thomas Assheton Smith III moved to Penton Lodge near Andover.
1828	Death of Assheton Smith II. Demolition of old house and rebuilding of present Tedworth House began.
1830	The newly built Tedworth House is completed. Assheton Smith III, probably the country's greatest foxhunter, moves in. He clears hundreds of square miles of land for hunting.
1834	Population of North Tidworth recorded as 392, South Tidworth as 217.
1845	Stables reported as having 50 horses. The kennels held a pack of 400 foxhounds for the Tedworth hunt. The conservatory was built.
1857	Mrs. Matilda Assheton Smith's school opened at Hampshire Cross.
1858	Thomas Assheton Smith II died without issue.
1859	Matilda Assheton Smith died, bequeathing the Tedworth estate to her nephew Francis Sloane Stanley.
1861	Lord Broughton, a famous statesman, living at Tedworth House as tenant of F. S. Stanley.
1870	Edward Studd, a retired planter, in occupation of house. Owner of a Grand National winner, he formed a racing establishment at Tedworth House. Following his religious conversion the house became a revivalist centre. His most famous son, Charlie (C. T.), was the leading English cricketer of his day. He later became a well-known missionary.
1876	Stanley family sold Tedworth House and estate to Sir John Kelk, a well-known building engineer, whose work included the Albert Memorial. The Studd family remained in residence until 1878.
1878	Extensive restructuring began on the house which was to last for two years, employing hundreds of workers.
1880	The new South Tidworth parish church of St Mary completed. Work finished on refurbishing of Tedworth House.
1897	House and estate sold to War Department. Queen Victoria's jubilee celebrated in village.
1898	Colonel R. M. Barklie took up residence as first military occupant.

1900	Maj. Gen. T. A. Cooke, commander of troops Salisbury Plain, became next military occupant.
1901	Military branch railway line opened into village to assist construction of new barracks.
1903	Sewage works constructed in Tidworth Park. Military cemetery laid out.
1904	The first troops began to move into newly-completed barracks.
1905	House became official residence of Lt. Gen. Sir Ian Hamilton, Commander-in-Chief Southern Command.
1907	Tidworth Military Hospital opened.
1909	Gen. Sir Charles Douglas in residence at house. Garrison Theatre opened.
1912	Senior officers' houses built in grounds of Tedworth House, named Clive, Havelock, Muir and Hastings House.
1913	Garrison power station built in Delhi Barracks, opening in 1914 to bring first electricity to the camp.
1915	From early part of W.W.1 Tedworth House became an Officer's Club – its primary role for the next 60 years.
1920	First Tidworth Tattoo held.
1925	New polo field (Fisher Ground) laid in Tedworth Park.
1942	U.S. troops arrived in village. House became an American Red Cross Club, run by Mrs. Theodore Roosevelt Jr.
1944	American troops depart to take part in D-Day landings.
1945–6	G.I.s returned to Tidworth, staging for the United States. Transit camp for G.I. brides at Perham Down.
1950s	Tedworth House reverted to an Officers' Club.
1951	Mausoleum in grounds conveyed to War Department for demolition.
1961	Garrison power station closed.
1963	Tidworth railway station closed. Track lifted the following year.
1977	Tidworth Military Hospital closed.
1978	Officers' Club closed. Tedworth House authorised to become a military Officers' Mess.

Appendix I: The Churches of Tidworth

Church of St Mary, South Tidworth

St Mary's, South Tidworth, is a church of unusual design (see Plate 12). It is seen on the left-hand side of the main road just after entering the village from Shipton Bellinger. It was the work of the reputable 19th-century architect John Johnson (1807–78) who had designed over a dozen churches in the Home Counties, but was probably best known for Alexandra Palace, London, which he rebuilt in 1875 after it was gutted by fire soon after opening. The central hall of the palace was one of the most impressive of all 19th-century structures. Johnson was commissioned by Sir John Kelk, the owner of Tedworth House, to build the new church near to the site of the medieval South Tidworth village church which had been demolished *c*.1784.

Johnson was never to see his very individual design completed; he died the year work started. The project was seen through by G. H. Gordon, the son of the canon of Salisbury Cathedral. The foundation stone was laid by Sir John Kelk's wife Rebecca Anne on 29 April 1879, the church being completed the following year. Built of rock-faced brown stone, its Gothic style gives it the appearance of a building much older than its late-Victorian date. The most striking feature of the church is the bell turret; emerging as a high-projecting mid-buttress in the west wall it becomes a round, tapered, highly elongated spire pointing sharply into the sky high above the pointed roof-line.

On entering the church by the south porch visitors are usually astonished at its internal dimensions which are far greater than seems possible from its external appearance. It is possibly deceptive because of its external height. The basic ground plan is a nave with aisles, a chancel and a south transept balanced on the north side by a vestry. An almost identical plan is found in the church of St Giles, Skelton, North Yorkshire, which is regarded as a perfect example of 13th-century design.

Below the short, high nave the roof is supported by the outstanding feature of this church – polished grey-veined marble columns with steeply rising half-arches surmounting each of the aisle bays. The sanctuary floor is of inlaid Italian mosaic, beautifully set off by the original highly-crafted wooden and brass furnishings to form an integrated whole. Quality detail is seen throughout in the sculpture, railings and capitals. The chancel has marble shafts inlaid into the three walls forming pilasters. Behind the altar the sculpted ornamental screen (reredos) lies below three beautiful, tall, stained-glass windows. There is a sculptured pulpit and font and further fine examples of stained-glass windows.

The church was declared redundant from 1 September 1972, passing the following year into the stewardship of the Redundant Churches Fund. This body was set up by Parliament in 1969 to maintain and preserve churches no longer needed for worship but which are of historic interest. Following the closure of St Mary's there was an ecclesiastical union of the North and South Tidworth parishes to form a 'new benefice and parish of Tidworth' under the Salisbury diocese. Holy Trinity, North Tidworth, then became the parish church. Interestingly, this union had been recommended by the parliamentary surveyors in 1650! A further union took place in 1987 with the inauguration of the United Benefice of Tidworth, Ludgershall and Faberstown. St James' church, Ludgershall, became the new parish church of the benefice.

St Mary's, South Tidworth, stands today as a grand example of Victorian architecture in the Gothic style, creating a dramatic entrance to the village. At the time of writing it could be visited by arrangement, details for obtaining the key being on the north door.

Holy Trinity church, North Tidworth

This church has served the village of North Tidworth since medieval times. Standing beside a group of old cottages in a tranquil setting, the brick-and-flint church reminds us of a bygone age when it was the centre of village life. There is a west tower, repaired in brick in 1600, a perpendicular nave and a chancel. Within the church an impressive board on one wall lists the rectors of North Tidworth from 1297, marking its continuous use over seven centuries. One rector, Edward Fraser Vaughan Williams, did much to restore the church following his appointment in 1868. He was the uncle of the famous British composer Ralph Vaughan Williams (1872–1958), who attended several services in Tidworth.

An earlier rector, Thomas Pierce, who was instituted to the parish in 1674, served about three years at North Tidworth before being made Dean of Salisbury. He appears to have been combative by nature and is said to have driven the Bishop of Sarum (now Salisbury), Seth Ward, to his death by engaging him in long and angry controversy. Thomas Pierce's son Robert became rector of the parish in 1680. A brass inscription on the belfry wall gives some detail of the Pierce family. Dean Thomas died on 28 March 1691 and was buried on the south side of the churchyard. His mother, who died in 1698, was buried beside him. Robert was laid to rest in the churchyard on 3 December 1707.

There is a peal of five bells in Holy Trinity church. The largest, a tenor, weighing approximately 10 cwt., was cast in 1809 by James Wells of Aldbourne. The treble was cast by Clement Tozier of Salisbury in 1700. The three remaining bells are the 2nd 'Be Joyful in God', the 3rd 'Sing Praise to God', and 4th 'O Praise the Lord', all cast in 1619 by John Wallis of Salisbury.

Church of St George and St Patrick (R.C.), North Tidworth

Pevsner and Lloyd (see Bibliography) provide only sparse detail of this church; little other information seems to exist. They record that it was built in 1912 from a design by G. L. W. Blount. The flint building is long and low with a short tower at the north-east end. Inside, the white walls provide a stark contrast to the complex thin, black timbers in the roof.

Garrison church of St Michael (C. of E.), South Tidworth

Designed by a London architect, Douglas Hoyland, this church was constructed by a local builder, Messrs. C. Grace & Sons of Ludgershall in 1912. Of no great architectural merit, the building is nonetheless of impressive size and fulfils an important function in providing a spacious place of worship for troops and their families. It was certainly a more ambitious project than that originally mooted, which was for a temporary corrugated-iron building. Begun in 1911 with the foundation stone being laid by the General Officer Commanding 3rd Division, Maj. Gen. Sir Henry Rawlinson, Bt., C.V.O., C.B., it was completed in only 12 months. On 4 May 1912 the Chaplain-General dedicated the church to St Michael in a ceremony attended by the Secretary of State for War Lord Haldane, the Bishop of Salisbury and all the Chief Officers on Salisbury Plain.

Constructed of buff-coloured hollow terracotta blocks, the church stands in the centre of the military garrison on rising ground overlooking Furze Hill on the other side of the valley. Groups of perpendicular windows surround the building at two levels. Over the crossing of the transept is a bell-tower surmounted with a spire. Much of the cost of the church was raised by public donation and regiments were asked to present funishings. The 18th Hussars gave the carved oak eagle lectern, whilst the oak font was presented by the

2nd Cavalry Brigade. Further furnishings were given by individuals, including donations from Gen. Sir Ian Hamilton.

Despite its relatively cheap construction, the garrison church of St Michael has weathered its first 80 years remarkably well and stands today as a sturdy, solid-looking building providing a haven of tranquillity amongst the bustle of regimental activity. Originally designed to seat a congregation of 1,000, the church now has a capacity of about eight hundred following various alterations and improvements, including enlargement of the sanctuary.

The Burial Chapel, Church Lane, South Tidworth

Standing in a secluded churchyard in the shadow of Furze Hill is the Burial or Mortuary Chapel, built of masonry from a church mentioned in Domesday Book. This small building is only about 22 feet long by 18 feet wide, but served well as the chapel for the Assheton Smith family of Tedworth House after the medieval South Tedworth church was demolished in 1784. Material from the demolished church was used to build the chapel which became the only place of worship in South Tedworth. Some records of 1850 refer to the Burial Chapel as South Tedworth church, indicating that it was used then, as later, as the general village church.

There is a west porch and doorway with belfry above, two small windows in the north and south walls, and a window of 14th-century design in the east wall. This well-proportioned window has three trefoil lights with two quatrefoils over a moulded label. Of great interest, on the north and south walls, are two ornate marble tablets dating from about 1730, which were removed from the old parish church during its demolition. The south tablet honours the memory of 'Speaker' John Smith and Lady Anne Smith of Tedworth House. The other is an epitaph to Lieutenant William Assheton Smith who died at sea in January 1806, just a few months after fighting in the Battle of Trafalgar.

Just a few yards to the north of the entrance porch lie the graves of Thomas Assheton Smith III, his wife Matilda and his sister Harriet. Considering the enormous wealth, influence and reputation of the Assheton Smiths, their graves are remarkably inconsequential.

South Tedworth parish church (now demolished)

The parish church of South Tedworth stood close to the present site of St Mary's church, South Tidworth, at the south entrance into the village. It was demolished in 1784 at the behest of Thomas Assheton Smith II. We know that the church was of medieval origin, receiving a mention in Domesday Book. It was 60 feet 2 inches in length and 22 feet 6 inches in width with a square tower, high nave, chancel and large porch in typical medieval fashion.

In 1784 a faculty was drawn up and signed by the Bishop of Winchester authorising Assheton Smith II to arrange its demolition and removal to another place. The faculty states that the parish church of South Tedworth:

> . . . is inconveniently situated near the Mansion House of Thomas Assheton Smith in a low, damp and unwholesome place and intercepts the view or prospect from the same House and is an old and decayed building and requires a considerable sum annually to be laid out in the repairs of it; that the said Thomas Assheton Smith is willing and desirous at his own expense to take down and remove the said Parish Church to the Work End of a certain piece of Glebe belonging to the said Rectory containing one acre, one rood and 35 perches . . . being a more dry, healthy and convenient situation . . .

In this document Assheton Smith is, interestingly, referred to as 'Lord of the Manor'. Following demolition the material was used to build the Burial Chapel still standing in

Church Lane, South Tidworth. Several marble tablets and monumental inscriptions were also removed and placed on the walls of the Burial Chapel.

The Mausoleum, Tedworth Park, South Tedworth (now demolished)

Once a fine feature of the Tedworth House estate, the mausoleum regrettably no longer exists. Completed soon after the death of Thomas Assheton Smith III in 1858, it stood at the far end of a path running west from Tedworth House, past a lovely stone fountain pool, through the wood known as The Plantation which still exists today. The mausoleum was an impressive domed building about fifty feet long and thirty wide, built of stone. It stood until the early 1950s when it was demolished by the War Office under an agreement with the Bishop of Winchester. It was conveyed to the War Office for a token sum of five pounds following a meeting of the Parochial Church Council in Tidworth, held on 18 October 1951, when it was agreed that, following a service of deconsecration, the building should be demolished. The coloured glass windows were to be handed over to the rector of South Tidworth, but their present whereabouts are unknown.

Presbyterian church of St Andrew and St Mark

This was the first church to be built in the Tidworth garrison area in response to the great increase in village population following the building of the barracks. Standing at the junction of St Patrick's Avenue and Kirkee Road, it opened for worship on Sunday 24 January 1909 under the Rev. W. S. Jaffray. Somewhat overshadowed by the building of the larger, better constructed garrison church of St Michael in 1912, it nevertheless served the garrison well until its closure in 1964.

Garrison church of St Andrew and St Mark

Worship for Church of Scotland, Methodist and Free Churches was allowed to continue after the closing of the Presbyterian church by the opening of part of the Ian Hamilton Wesleyan Soldiers' Home which became the garrison church of St Andrew and St Mark. This church existed for only about twenty years, closing in September 1985 when services were transferred to St Michael's on an inter-denominational basis.

Appendix II: The Three Graces

The saloon or great hall in Tedworth House has at times been known as the 'Graces Hall', overlooked as it is by a plaster copy of Canova's famous three-figured statue (see Plate 15). The actual date the statue was placed in its alcove on the ornate grand staircase is not known. There is no mention of it in Eardley-Wilmot's account (1859) of the life of Thomas Assheton Smith, who arranged the building of the present house, but in 1897 the statue was put up for sale as part of the house contents. There is no record of its actual sale at that time, although it may have been purchased and then presented back. It was possibly bought for the house during the major refurbishment by John Kelk in 1878–80 when much work was done on the central saloon. Questions are often asked about the original work so some detail is given below.

The Italian sculptor Antonio Canova (1757–1822) became a leading exponent of the neo-classical style, producing exquisite statues and bas-reliefs for leading people of his day. It is said that his talent was first brought to notice when he carved a lion in butter. He was originally commissioned to produce *The Three Graces* by the 6th Duke of Bedford, who was visiting Rome, in 1814. The following year Canova was invited to Woburn Abbey to advise on its placement. A special Temple of the Graces was erected in the grounds of Woburn Abbey to house the statue which was delivered in 1817. It stood in the Temple for the next 168 years.

In Greek mythology the Graces, or Charities as they were also known, were three goddesses who personified light, joy and fertility. They inspired the arts, sciences and all things graceful. Named Agalia, Thalia and Euphrosyne, they were the daughters of Zeus and the oceanid nymph Eurynome. The original *Three Graces* was displayed at Woburn until 1985 when it was sold to an investment company operating in the Cayman Islands. Due to be sold to the Getty Museum in the U.S.A. in March 1990 for about £7.6 million, it became the centre of a major campaign to save it for the nation. Even H.R.H. the Prince of Wales lent his support to keep it in Britain. The export licence was revoked by the Government whilst other buyers were asked to bid. At the time of writing the original Canova statue was still awaiting acceptance of a bid by a potential buyer.

Appendix III: The Sale of Tedworth House, 1897

The circumstances leading to the sale of Tedworth House to the War Department in 1897 for the sum of £95,000 have been outlined in the first section of Part Three under the heading 'Military Manoeuvres'. This appendix examines the sale in more detail, particularly in relation to the layout of the house at that time as described in the sale documents.

The sale by private contract was arranged by Messrs. Daniel Smith, Son and Oakley of Pall Mall, London, who issued a brochure, the cover of which is illustrated in Plate 17. The figure of 6,618 acres printed on the cover was altered in manuscript on the original document, after final assessment, to read 6,616 acres, 2 roods, 31 perches. This included the whole of the parishes of North and South Tedworth (except a few glebe fields), Perham Down and a large part of the village of Shipton Bellinger to the south. The Tedworth estate was described as lying in a 'First-Class Sporting and Residential District, capable of producing a large Game'. It was well organised for the rearing and preservation of game including partridge, pheasant and covert shooting. Some indication of the extent of sport available is given in a statement of the game killed on the estate during the 1892–3 season: 2,767 pheasants, 916 partridges, 805 hares, 10,117 rabbits and 4 woodcock, a total of 14,609 head.

The house itself is described as being charmingly situated in a well-sheltered position, its southern aspects overlooking a fine undulating and well-timbered park of some 300 acres, affording beautiful views across to high hills topped with woods and plantations on either side. The approach to the house was from the Lodge entrance along a drive running through the park and pleasure grounds. The mansion was said to be a 'Noble and Modern Residence, excellently and substantially built with all Portland Stone fronts, and well designed and executed with every attention to the requirements of a Nobleman's Large Establishment'. It had an attractive approach with a large stone *porte-cochère*, a long conservatory, a corridor and a palm house. House lighting was by gas from the private works next to Home Farm.

The reception rooms on the ground floor were handsomely decorated and well arranged around the fine and lofty central saloon. The saloon and reception rooms were approached, as today, by the large outer hall with its fine inlaid mantelpiece with over-mantel. A lobby, lavatory and vestibule lead out from the outer hall. By comparing measurements on the sale documents with the dimensions of the rooms today the author has been able to discover the original names and uses of the main rooms on the ground floor. The three interlinked reception rooms to the left on entering the outer hall, which are today known as the function room, ballroom and green room, were listed in the sales brochure of 1897 as the billiard room, drawing room and library. From this library a small ante-room led to the dining room (now rather confusingly known as the library).

This dining room is the one relic of the earlier house retained during the rebuilding of 1830. The sale documents describe it as a handsome room with panelled oak dado, oak panels on the wall and hung with figured brown silk damask. The panelling remains unchanged today and, together with a splendid and delicately crafted chandelier and fine fireplace, gives the room an elegant character. Leading from the other side of the dining room was another ante-room (now a bar), then a 'gentlemen's room' with adjoining gun room (now an ante-room and bar respectively). Immediately opposite the gun room was the butler's pantry with built-in strong-room; this was being used at the time of writing as a television room. Next to the ante-room was a study (now a dining room) with strong-room, lavatory and water closet. A private staircase led from the study to the owner's best bedroom, although no sign of it remains today. Finally, at the end of that wing was a boudoir (now the breakfast room) leading into an open-sided gallery, or loggia, which was used on fine days as a sitting room.

On the first floor were 13 best bedrooms and dressing rooms and two smaller ones, all of which were approached from the central saloon by the grand staircase. A separate staircase led to the servants' rooms, which included nine servants' bedrooms in the north wing and 10 good visitors' and bachelors' rooms, as well as various lobbies and bathrooms.

In the ground floor of the north wing, beneath the servants' bedrooms, were the domestic offices, butler's room, housekeeper's room, various stores and the kitchen. In the yard detached from the north wing was a block, largely unchanged today, comprising a wash house, laundry and drying room with a coal yard, knife and wood house, cold meat larder and empty bottle house. Adjoining the block was the large walled drying area, now a garden. Behind this the covered tennis court could be approached from the house by a flight of steps to a door at the upper level leading on to a balcony. The tennis court, now a listed building, was also used in the winter as a skating rink.

The 'Capital Stabling' in the large block at the top of Stables Road provided accommodation for 21 horses, and rough stabling for five more. It also included a harness room, saddle room, three washing houses, a large coach house, open cart sheds, spacious lofts and accommodation for seven men together with two sets of living and mess rooms. Halfway up Stables Road a set of gates, now listed, led into the kitchen gardens which included vineries, greenhouses, hot houses and ferneries. Adjoining the gardens was a head gardener's cottage.

Of the farms sold as part of the Tedworth estate the more important were:

The Home Farm, 610 acres, South Tedworth/Shipton Bellinger
South Manor Farm, 1,139, North/South Tedworth
Warren Farm, 598 acres, South Tedworth/Shipton Bellinger
Shipton Manor Farm, 370 acres, Shipton Bellinger
Shipton Parsonage Farm, 499 acres, Shipton Bellinger
Zouch Farm, 692 acres, North Tedworth
Manor Farm, 692 acres, North Tedworth
Tedworth Down Farm, 635 acres, North Tedworth

To the south side of Home Farm were the kennels and stables of the Tedworth Hunt, together with a paddock and huntsman's house. In addition to these properties the estate also comprised numerous cottages, small holdings, the North Tedworth post office and blacksmith's shop and the *Ram Inn*, as well as the blacksmith's shop in Shipton Bellinger.

Bibliography

Allison, W. and Fairley, J., *The Monocled Mutineer* (1978)

Anstruther, I., *The Scandal of the Andover Workhouse* (1973)

Bettey, J. H., *Wessex From 1000 A.D.* (1986)

British Sports and Sportsmen – Hunting (1912)

British Sports and Sportsmen – Past and Present (1908)

Carpenter Turner, B., *A History of Hampshire* (1978)

Carver, F.M. Sir Michael (ed.), *The War Lords* (1976)

Cohen, Daniel, *Encyclopedia of Ghosts* (1989)

Cole, Lt. Col. Howard N., *The Story of Aldershot* (1980)

Cobbett, William, *Rural Rides* (1830)

Creagh, Sir O'Moore, *The V.C. & D.S.O.* (1918)

Domesday Book – Hampshire (1982)

Domesday Book – Wiltshire (1979)

Eardley Wilmot, Sir John E., *Reminiscences of the Late Thomas Assheton Smith, Esq.* (1860)

Fairbairns Book of Crests, Vol. 1 (1984)

Ffrench Blake, Lt. Col. R. L. V., *History of the 17th/21st Lancers, 1922–1959* (1962)

Grubb, Norman P., *C. T. Studd – Cricketer and Pioneer* (1970)

Hamilton, Ian B. M., *The Happy Warrior* (1966)

Hamilton, Lt. Gen. Sir Ian, *A Staff Officer's Scrap Book, Vols 1 & 2* (1905 & 1907)

History, Gazetteer & Directory of Hampshire (1878)

James, N. D. G., *Plain Soldiering* (1987)

Kelly's Directory of Hampshire (1899)

Maloney, J., 'Notes on the History of Tidworth' (unpublished)

Pevsner & Lloyd, *The Buildings of England – Hampshire and the Isle of Wight* (1967)

Roosevelt Jr., Mrs. Theodore, *Day Before Yesterday* (1959)

Shore, T. W., *A History of Hampshire* (1892)

The Victoria History of the Counties of England – Hampshire & the Isle of Wight (1911)

The Victoria History of the Counties of England – Wiltshire (1911)

Index